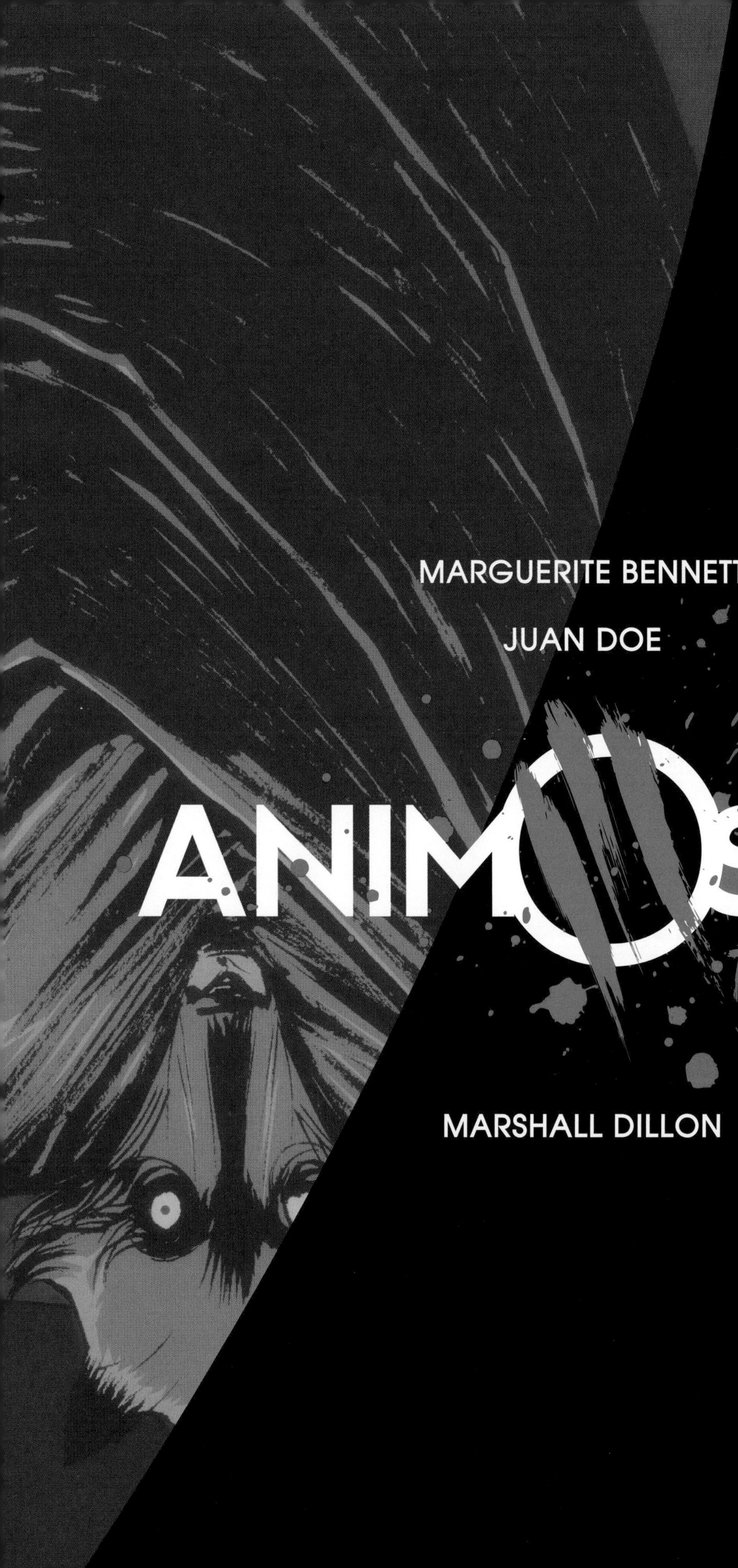

MARGUERITE BENNETT

JUAN DOE

ANIMOSITY™
THE RISE

MARSHALL DILLON

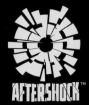

AFTERSHOCK™

ANIMOSITY
THE RISE

MARGUERITE BENNETT creator & writer

JUAN DOE artist

MARSHALL DILLON letterer

JUAN DOE front & original series covers

JOHN J. HILL logo designer

CHARLES PRITCHETT production

MIKE MARTS editor

AFTERSHOCK™

MIKE MARTS - Editor-in-Chief • JOE PRUETT - Publisher/ Chief Creative Officer • LEE KRAMER - President
JAWAD QURESHI - SVP, Investor Relations • JON KRAMER - Chief Executive Officer • MIKE ZAGARI - SVP, Brand
JAY BEHLING - Chief Financial Officer • STEPHAN NILSON - Publishing Operations Manager
LISA Y. WU - Retailer/Fan Relations Manager • ASHLEY WYATT - Publishing Assistant

AfterShock Trade Dress and Interior Design by JOHN J. HILL • AfterShock Logo Design by COMICRAFT
Original series production by CHARLES PRITCHETT • Proofreading by DOCTOR Z.
Publicity: contact AARON MARION (aaron@fifteenminutes.com) &
RYAN CROY (ryan@fifteenminutes.com) at 15 MINUTES
Special thanks to SVEN LARSEN, TEDDY LEO & LISA MOODY

First Printing: November 2017. 10 9 8 7 6 5 4 3 2 1

AFTERSHOCKCOMICS.COM Follow us on social media

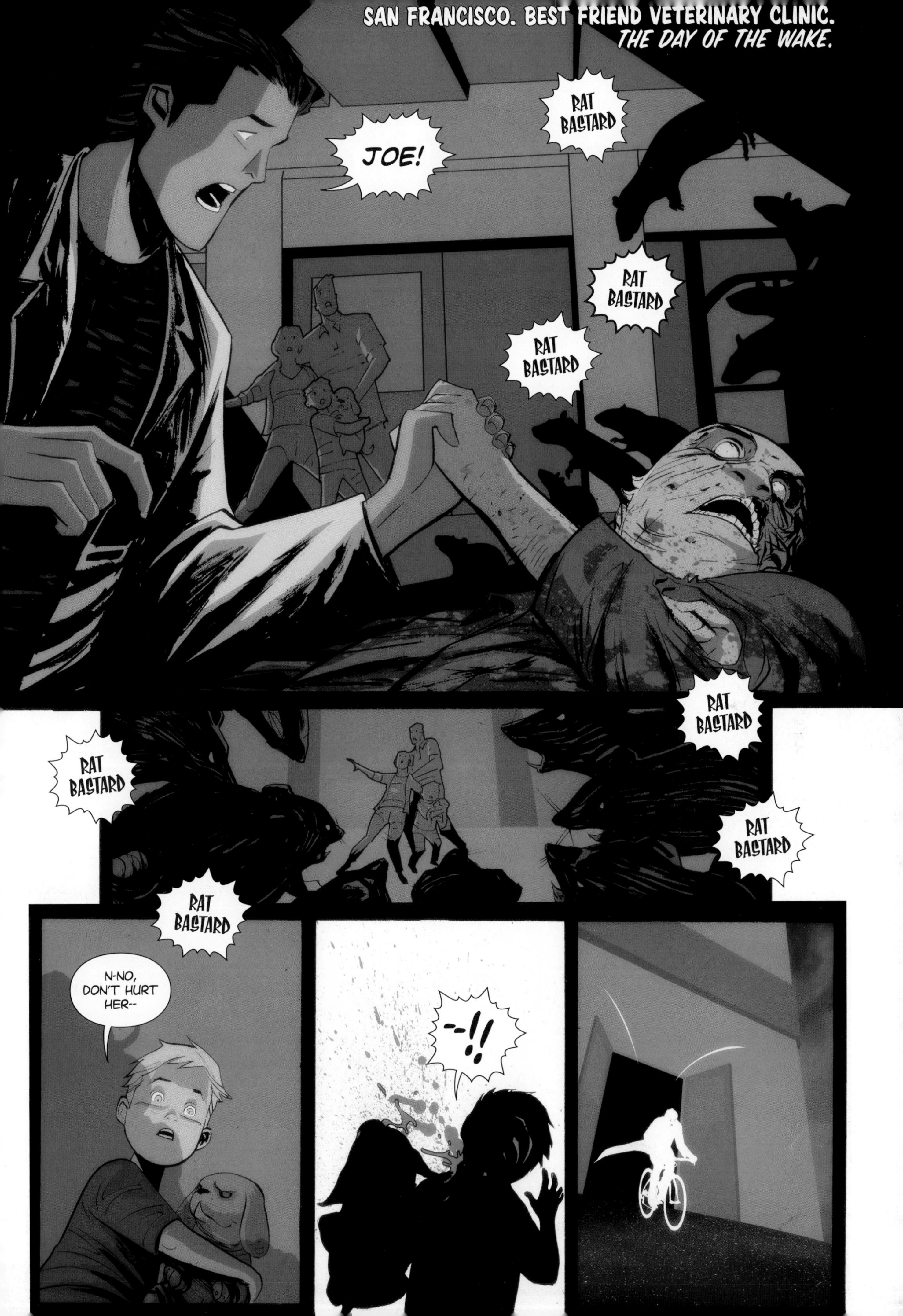
SAN FRANCISCO. BEST FRIEND VETERINARY CLINIC.
THE DAY OF THE WAKE.
JOE!
RAT BASTARD
RAT BASTARD
RAT BASTARD
RAT BASTARD
RAT BASTARD
RAT BASTARD
RAT BASTARD
N-NO, DON'T HURT HER--
--!!

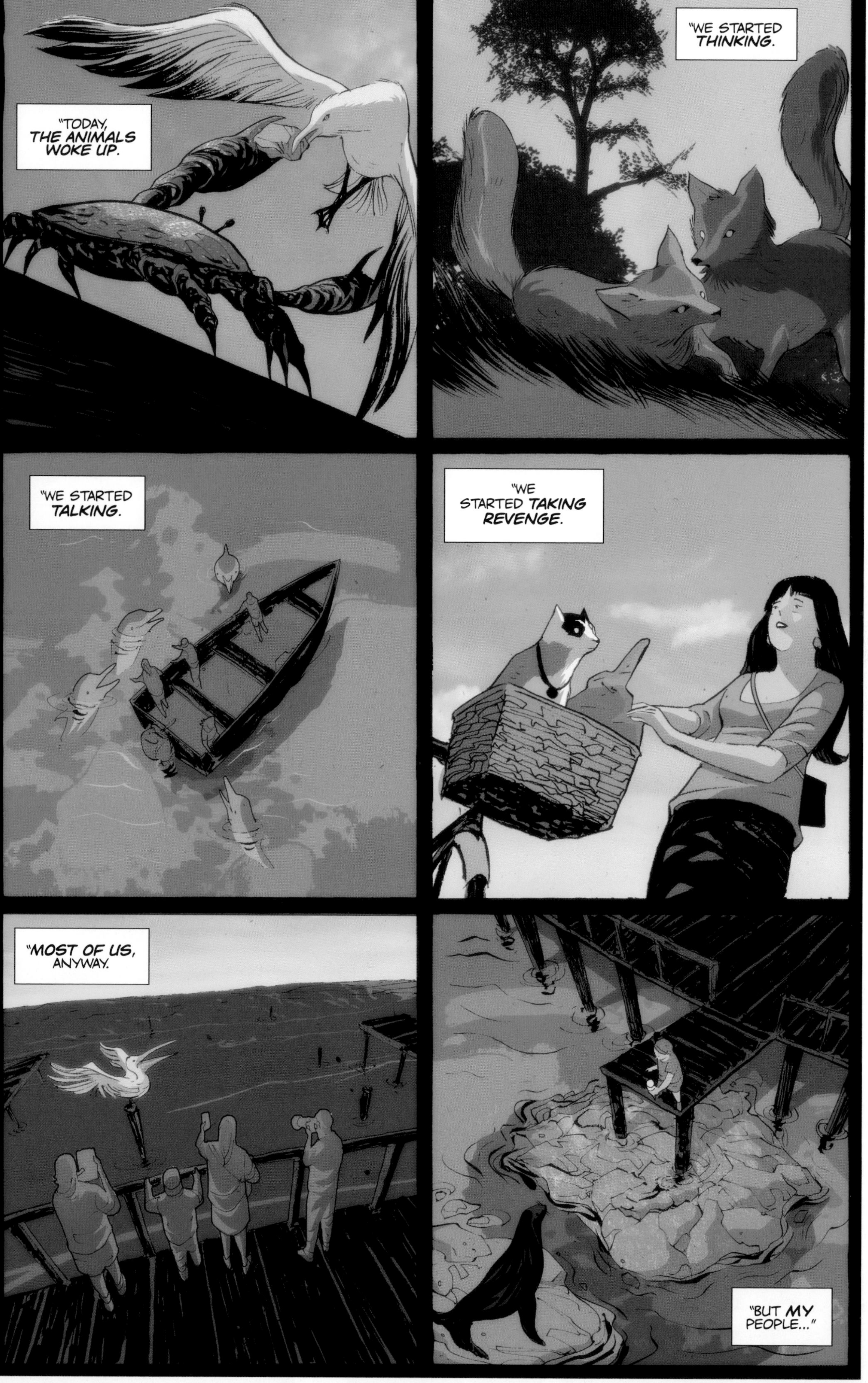
"TODAY, THE ANIMALS WOKE UP.
"WE STARTED THINKING.
"WE STARTED TALKING.
"WE STARTED TAKING REVENGE.
"MOST OF US, ANYWAY.
"BUT MY PEOPLE..."

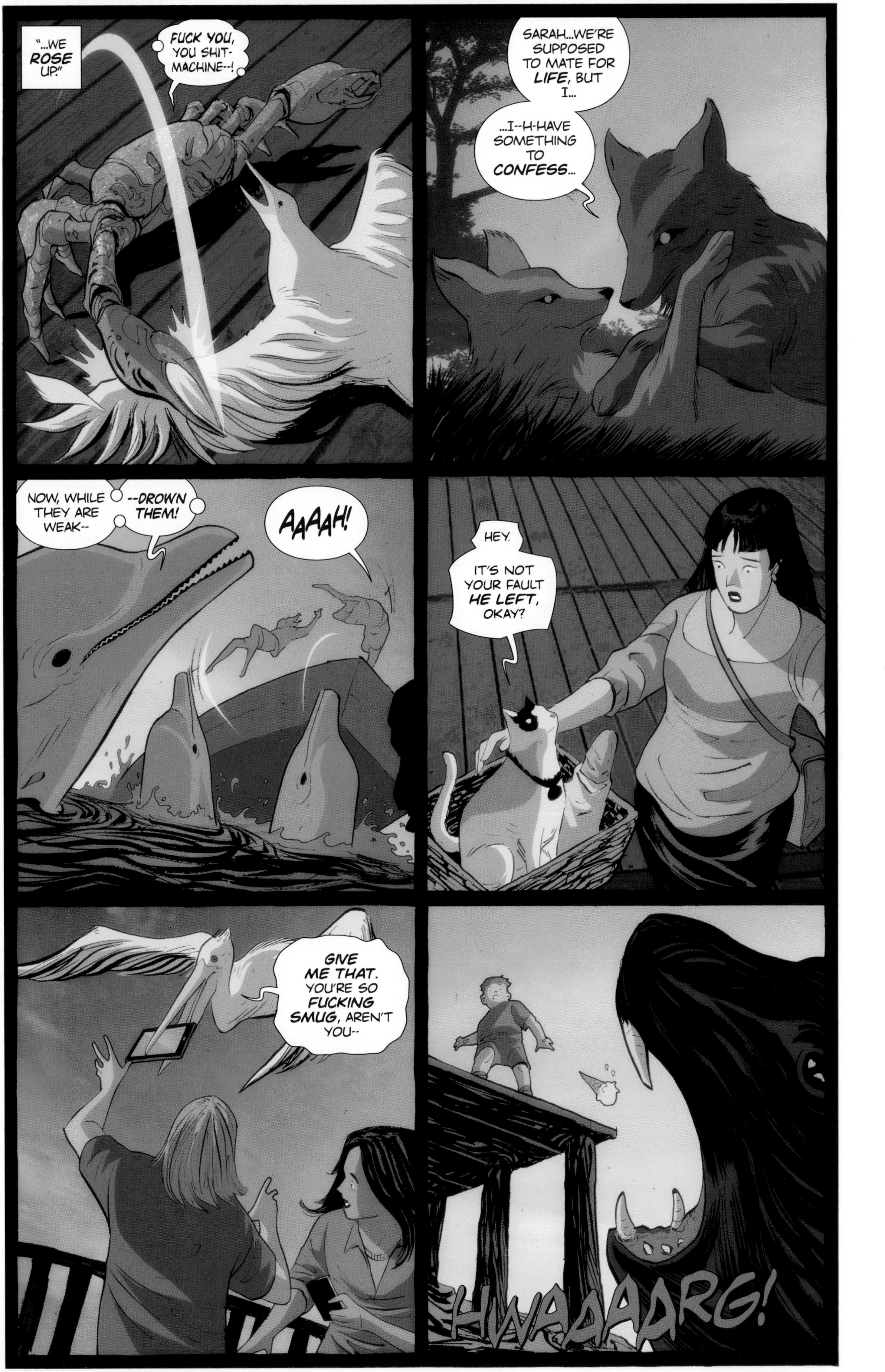
"...WE ROSE UP."
FUCK YOU, YOU SHIT-MACHINE--!
SARAH...WE'RE SUPPOSED TO MATE FOR LIFE, BUT I...
...I--H-HAVE SOMETHING TO CONFESS...
NOW, WHILE THEY ARE WEAK--
--DROWN THEM!
AAAAH!
HEY.
IT'S NOT YOUR FAULT HE LEFT, OKAY?
GIVE ME THAT. YOU'RE SO FUCKING SMUG, AREN'T YOU--
HWAAAARG!

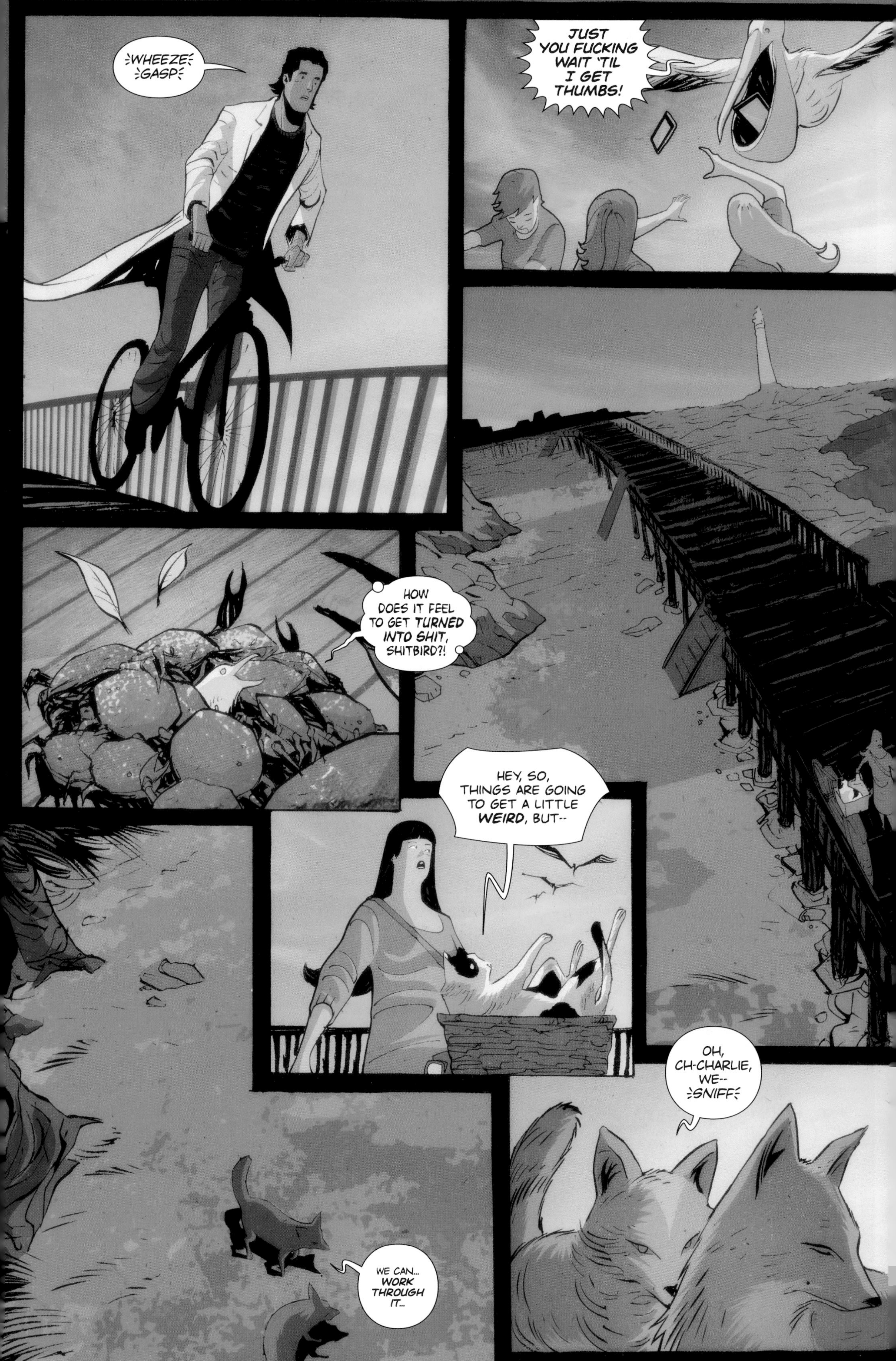

WHEEZE GASP
JUST YOU FUCKING WAIT 'TIL I GET THUMBS!
HOW DOES IT FEEL TO GET TURNED INTO SHIT, SHITBIRD?!
HEY, SO, THINGS ARE GOING TO GET A LITTLE WEIRD, BUT--
OH, CH-CHARLIE, WE-- SNIFF
WE CAN... WORK THROUGH IT...

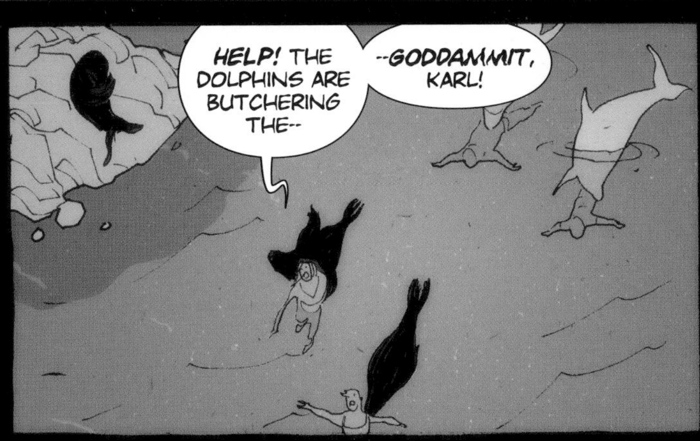
HELP! THE DOLPHINS ARE BUTCHERING THE--
--GODDAMMIT, KARL!
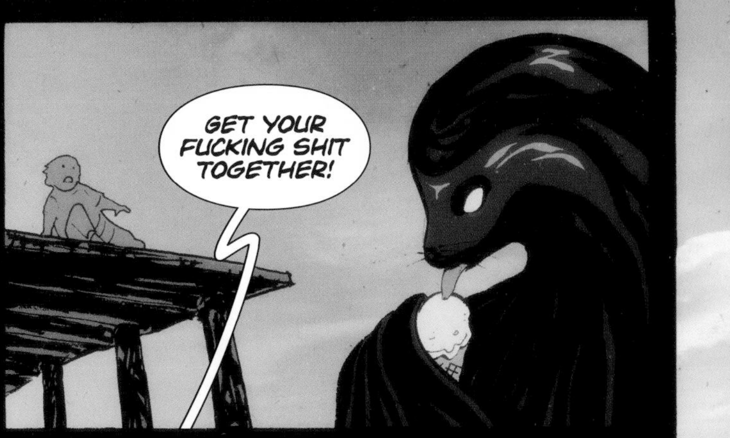
GET YOUR FUCKING SHIT TOGETHER!
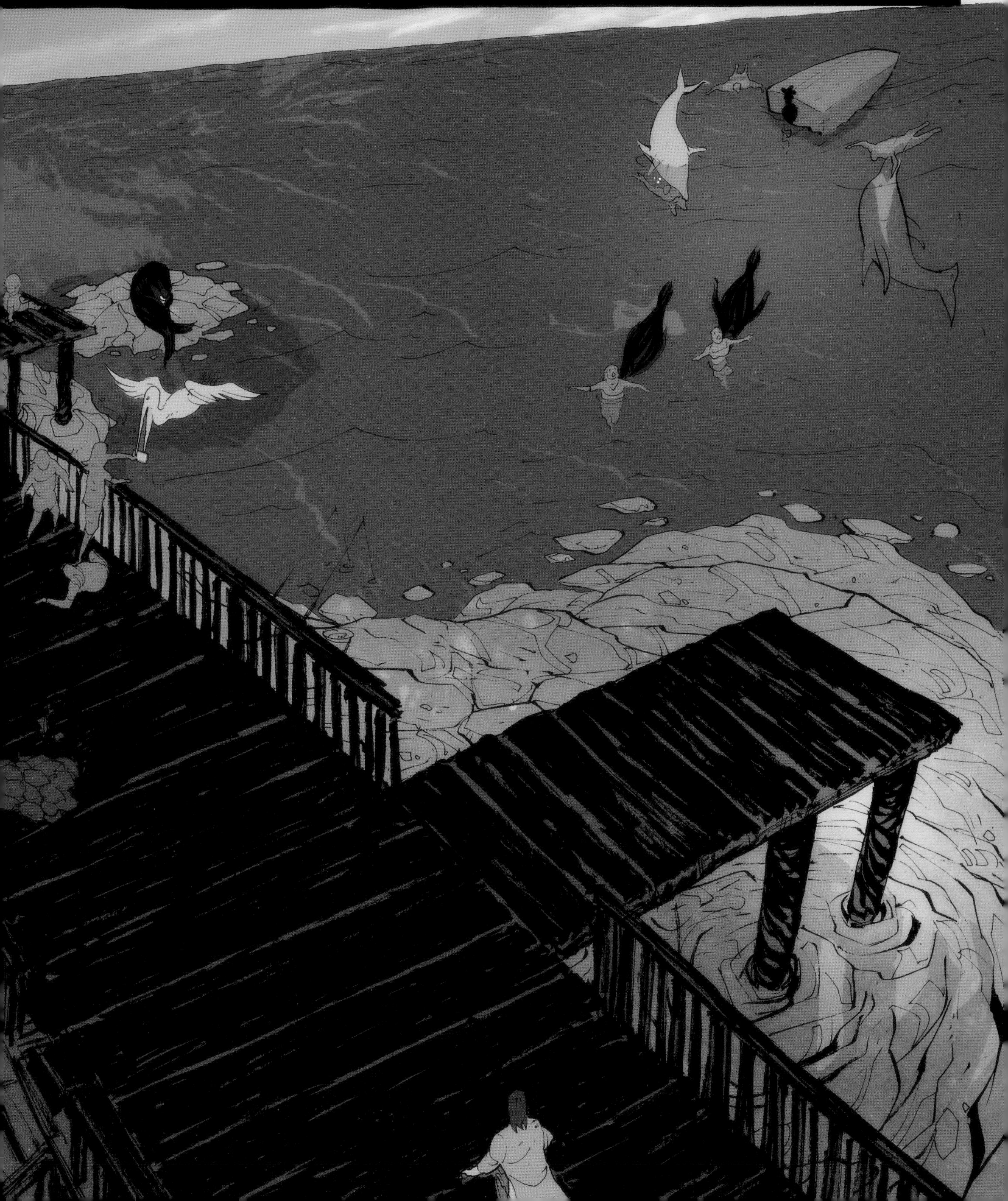

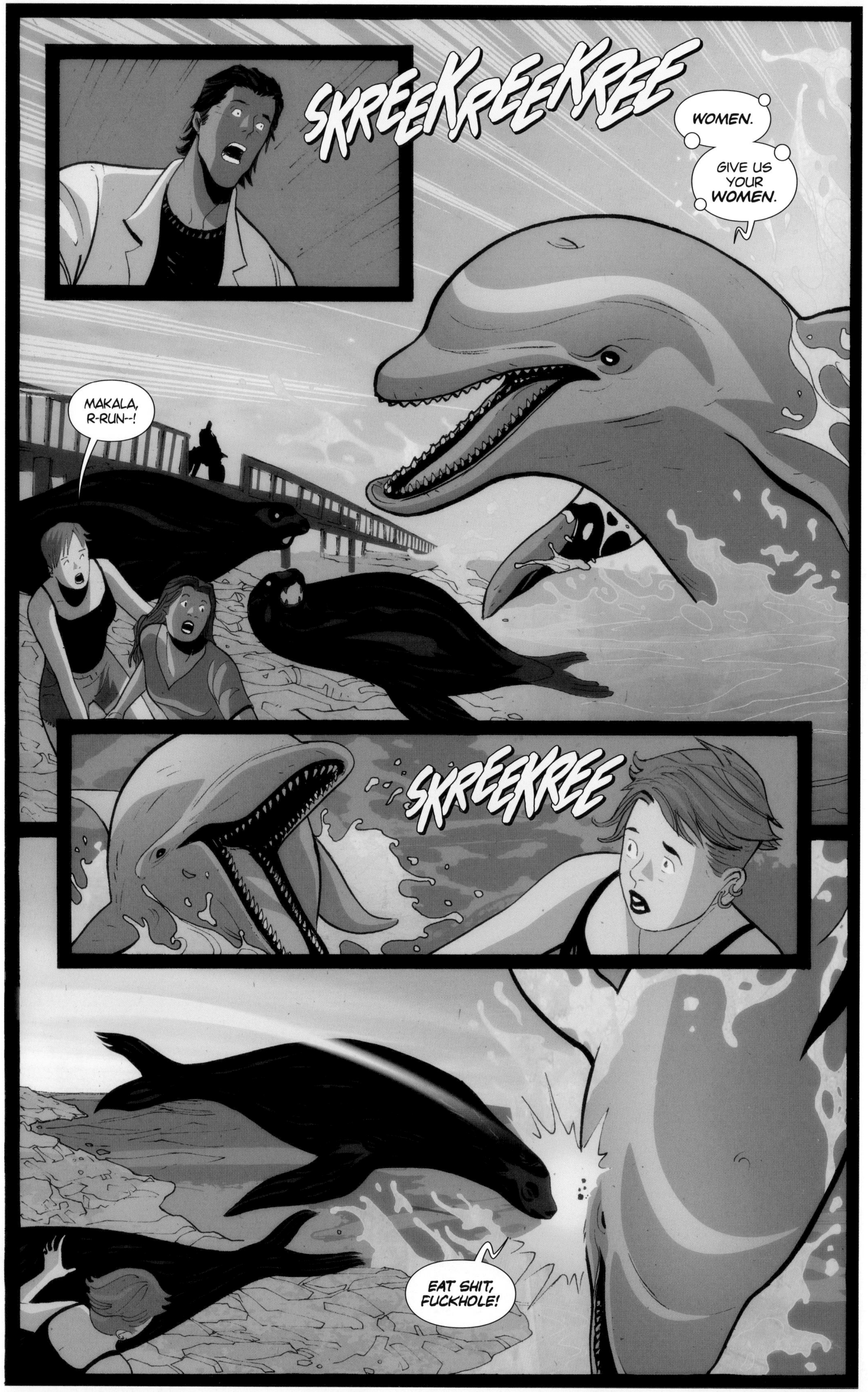
SKREEKREEKREE
WOMEN.
GIVE US YOUR WOMEN.
MAKALA, R-RUN--!
SKREEKREE
EAT SHIT, FUCKHOLE!

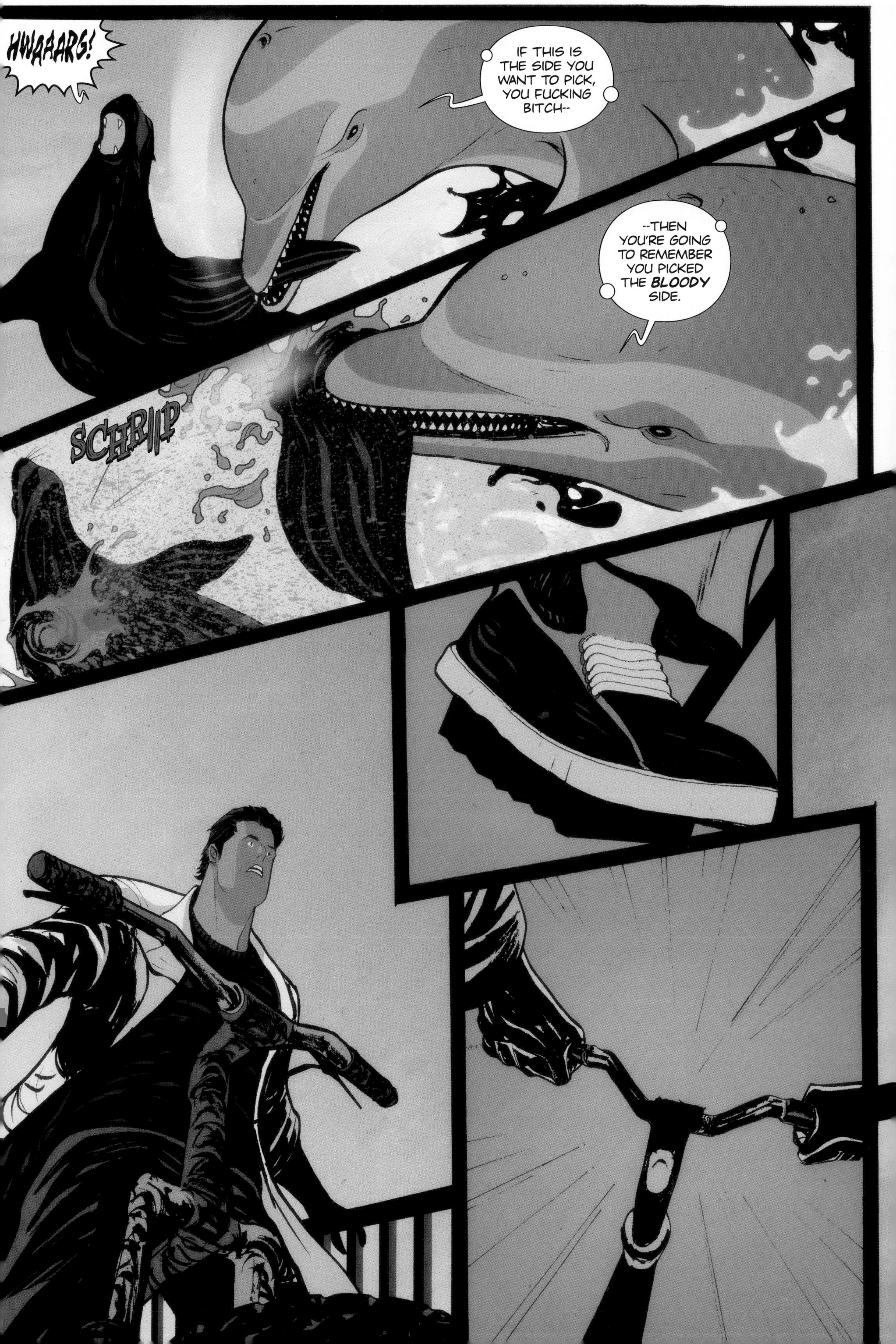
HWAAARG!
IF THIS IS THE SIDE YOU WANT TO PICK, YOU FUCKING BITCH--
--THEN YOU'RE GOING TO REMEMBER YOU PICKED THE BLOODY SIDE.
SCHRIIP

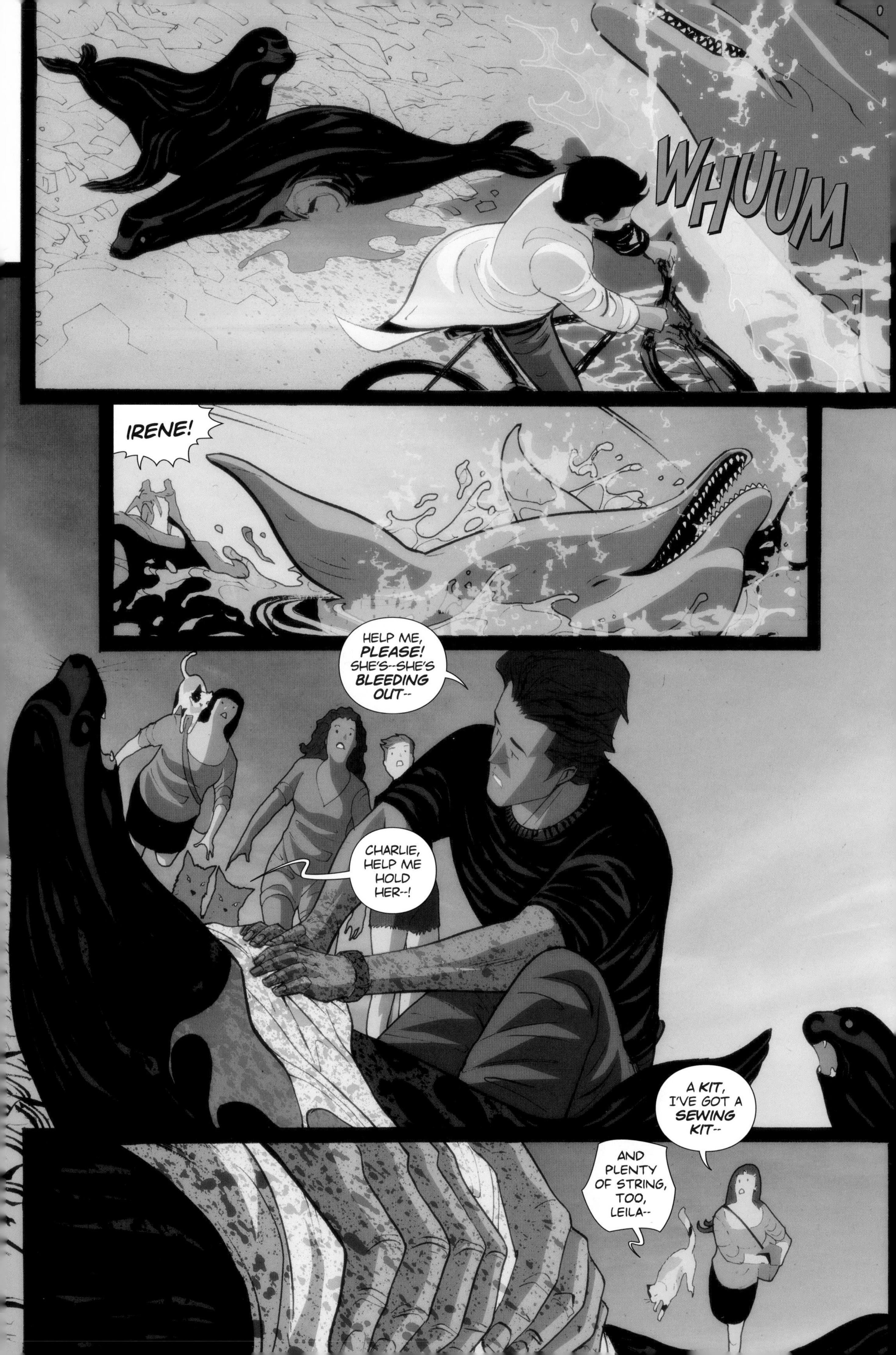
WHUUM
IRENE!
HELP ME, PLEASE! SHE'S--SHE'S BLEEDING OUT--
CHARLIE, HELP ME HOLD HER--!
A KIT, I'VE GOT A SEWING KIT--
AND PLENTY OF STRING, TOO, LEILA--

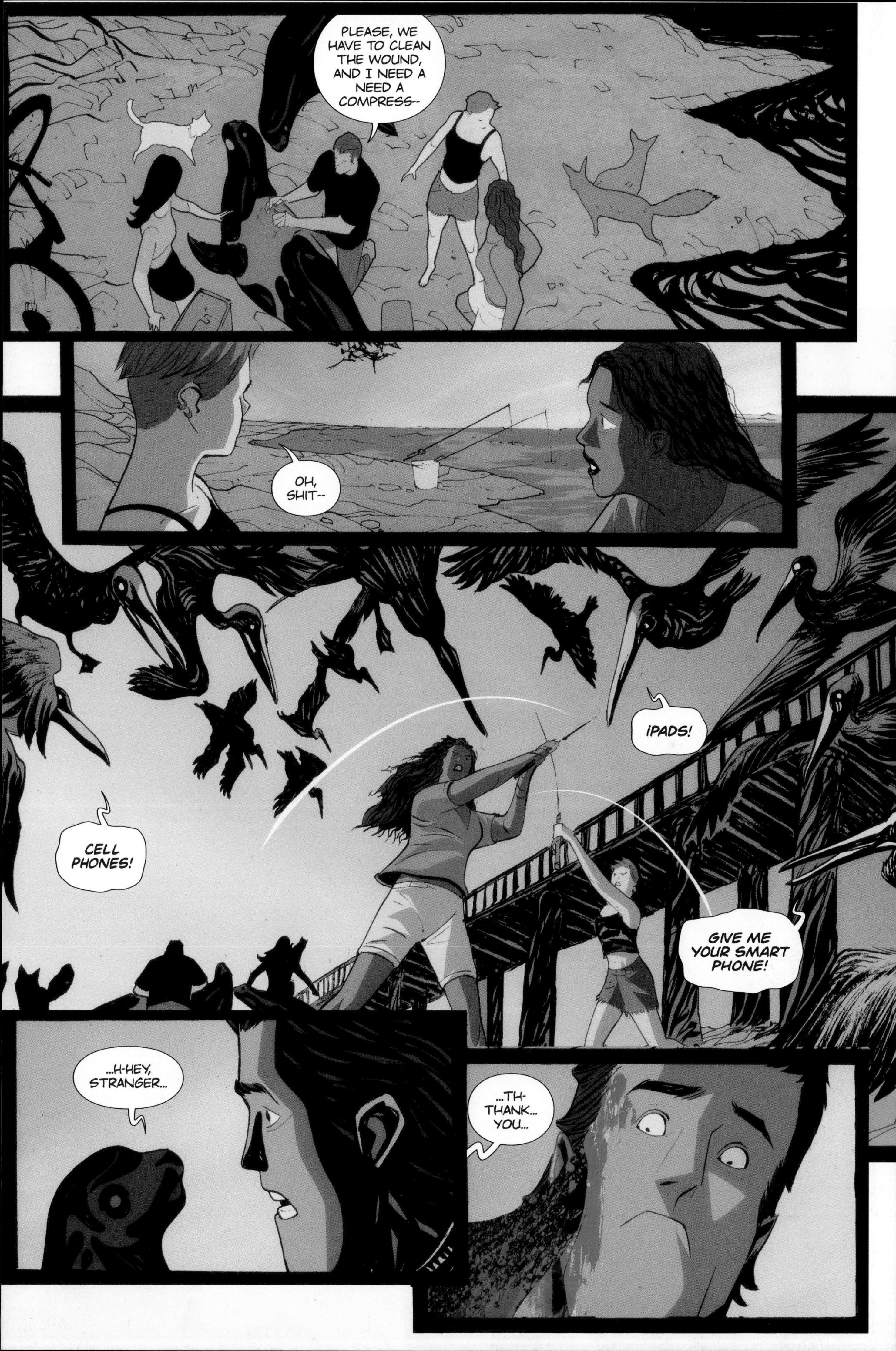
PLEASE, WE HAVE TO CLEAN THE WOUND, AND I NEED A NEED A COMPRESS--
OH, SHIT--
¡PADS!
CELL PHONES!
GIVE ME YOUR SMART PHONE!
...H-HEY, STRANGER...
...TH-THANK... YOU...

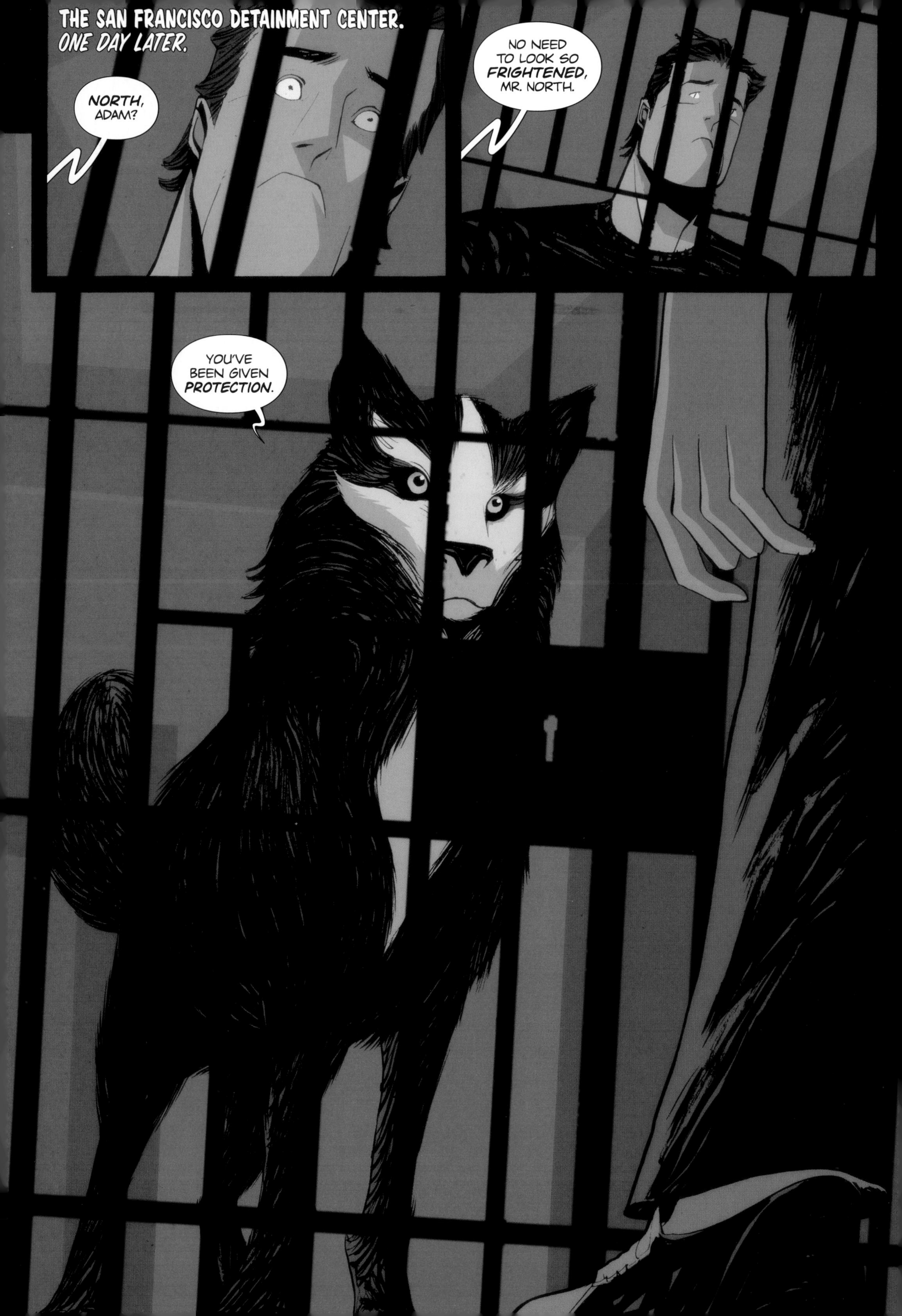
THE SAN FRANCISCO DETAINMENT CENTER. ONE DAY LATER.
NORTH, ADAM?
NO NEED TO LOOK SO FRIGHTENED, MR. NORTH.
YOU'VE BEEN GIVEN PROTECTION.

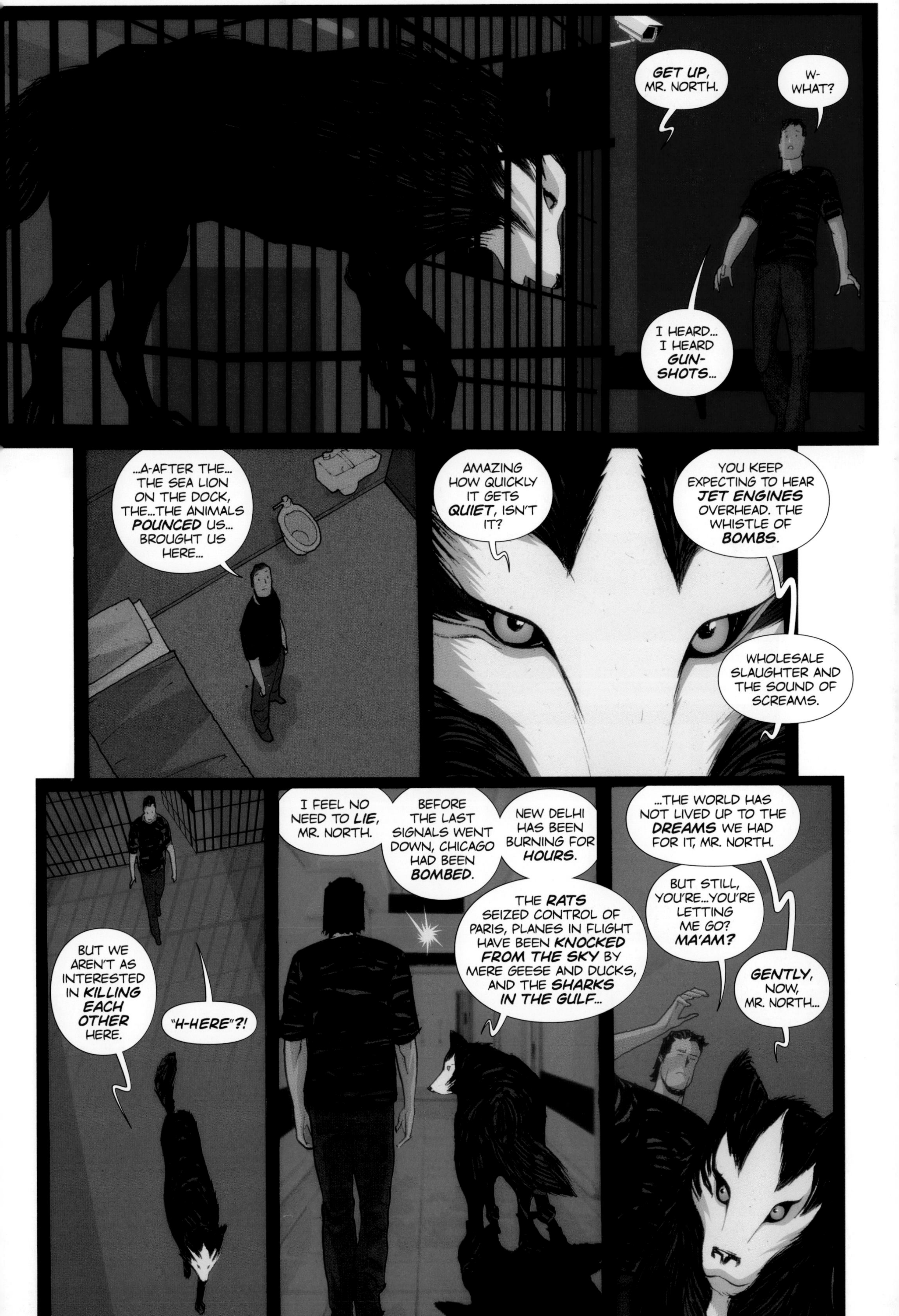
GET UP, MR. NORTH.
W- WHAT?
I HEARD... I HEARD GUN-SHOTS...
...A-AFTER THE... THE SEA LION ON THE DOCK, THE...THE ANIMALS POUNCED US... BROUGHT US HERE...
AMAZING HOW QUICKLY IT GETS QUIET, ISN'T IT?
YOU KEEP EXPECTING TO HEAR JET ENGINES OVERHEAD. THE WHISTLE OF BOMBS.
WHOLESALE SLAUGHTER AND THE SOUND OF SCREAMS.
BUT WE AREN'T AS INTERESTED IN KILLING EACH OTHER HERE.
"H-HERE"?!
I FEEL NO NEED TO LIE, MR. NORTH.
BEFORE THE LAST SIGNALS WENT DOWN, CHICAGO HAD BEEN BOMBED.
NEW DELHI HAS BEEN BURNING FOR HOURS.
THE RATS SEIZED CONTROL OF PARIS, PLANES IN FLIGHT HAVE BEEN KNOCKED FROM THE SKY BY MERE GEESE AND DUCKS, AND THE SHARKS IN THE GULF...
...THE WORLD HAS NOT LIVED UP TO THE DREAMS WE HAD FOR IT, MR. NORTH.
BUT STILL, YOU'RE...YOU'RE LETTING ME GO? MA'AM?
GENTLY, NOW, MR. NORTH...

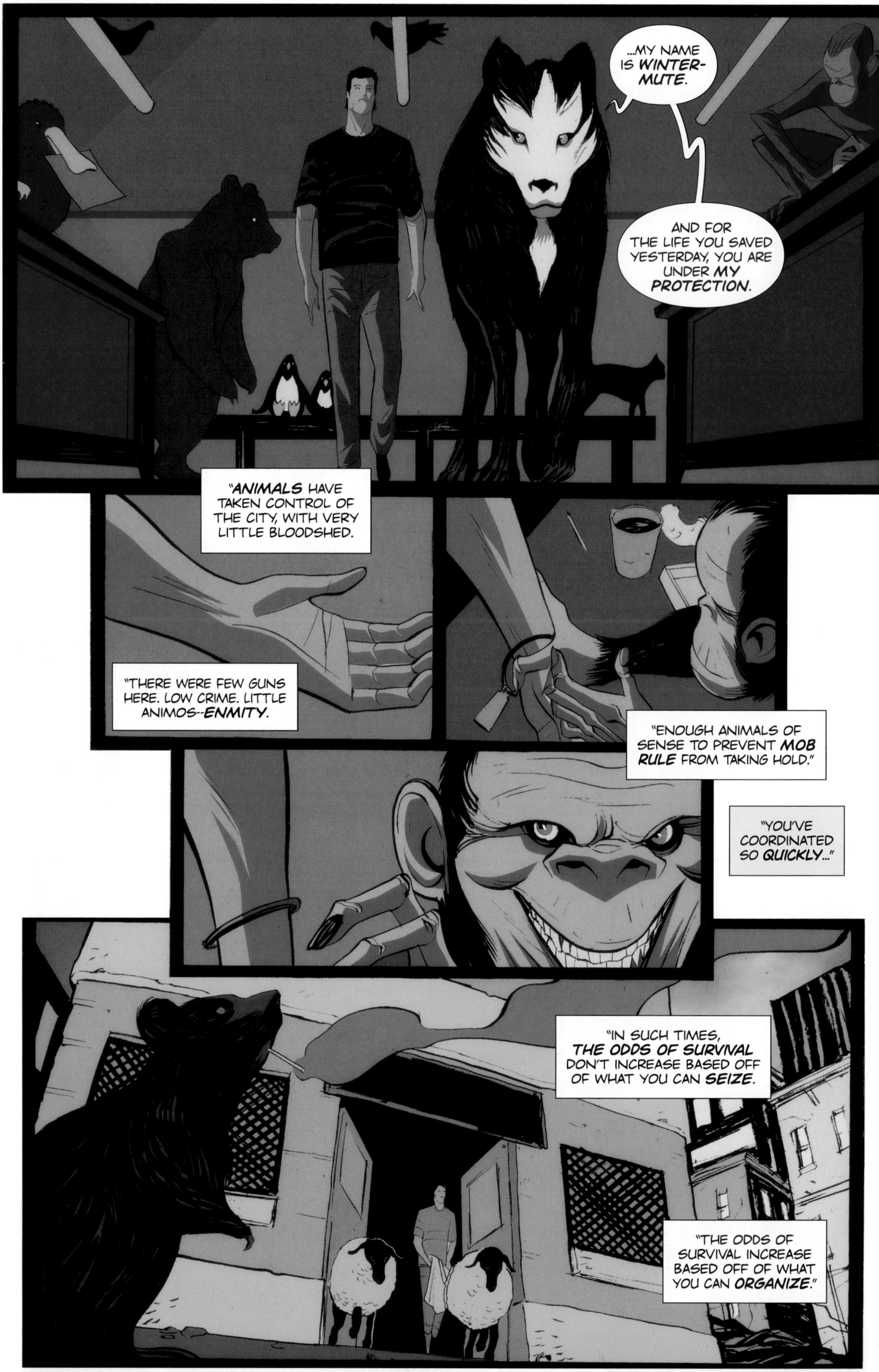
...MY NAME IS WINTER-MUTE.
AND FOR THE LIFE YOU SAVED YESTERDAY, YOU ARE UNDER MY PROTECTION.
"ANIMALS HAVE TAKEN CONTROL OF THE CITY, WITH VERY LITTLE BLOODSHED.
"THERE WERE FEW GUNS HERE. LOW CRIME. LITTLE ANIMOS--ENMITY.
"ENOUGH ANIMALS OF SENSE TO PREVENT MOB RULE FROM TAKING HOLD."
"YOU'VE COORDINATED SO QUICKLY..."
"IN SUCH TIMES, THE ODDS OF SURVIVAL DON'T INCREASE BASED OFF OF WHAT YOU CAN SEIZE.
"THE ODDS OF SURVIVAL INCREASE BASED OFF OF WHAT YOU CAN ORGANIZE."

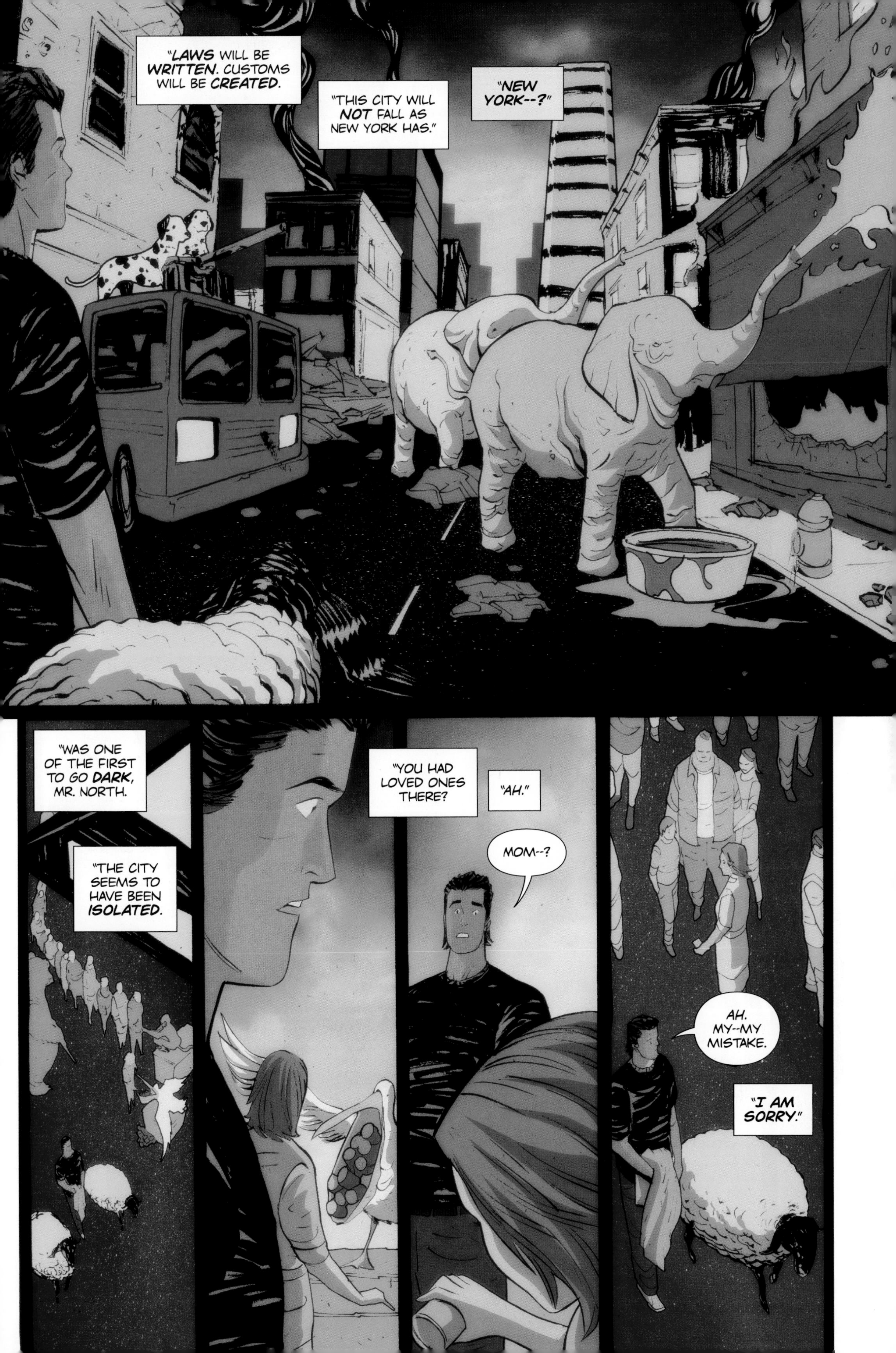
"LAWS WILL BE WRITTEN. CUSTOMS WILL BE CREATED.
"THIS CITY WILL NOT FALL AS NEW YORK HAS."
"NEW YORK--?"
"WAS ONE OF THE FIRST TO GO DARK, MR. NORTH.
"THE CITY SEEMS TO HAVE BEEN ISOLATED.
"YOU HAD LOVED ONES THERE?
"AH."
MOM--?
AH. MY--MY MISTAKE.
"I AM SORRY."

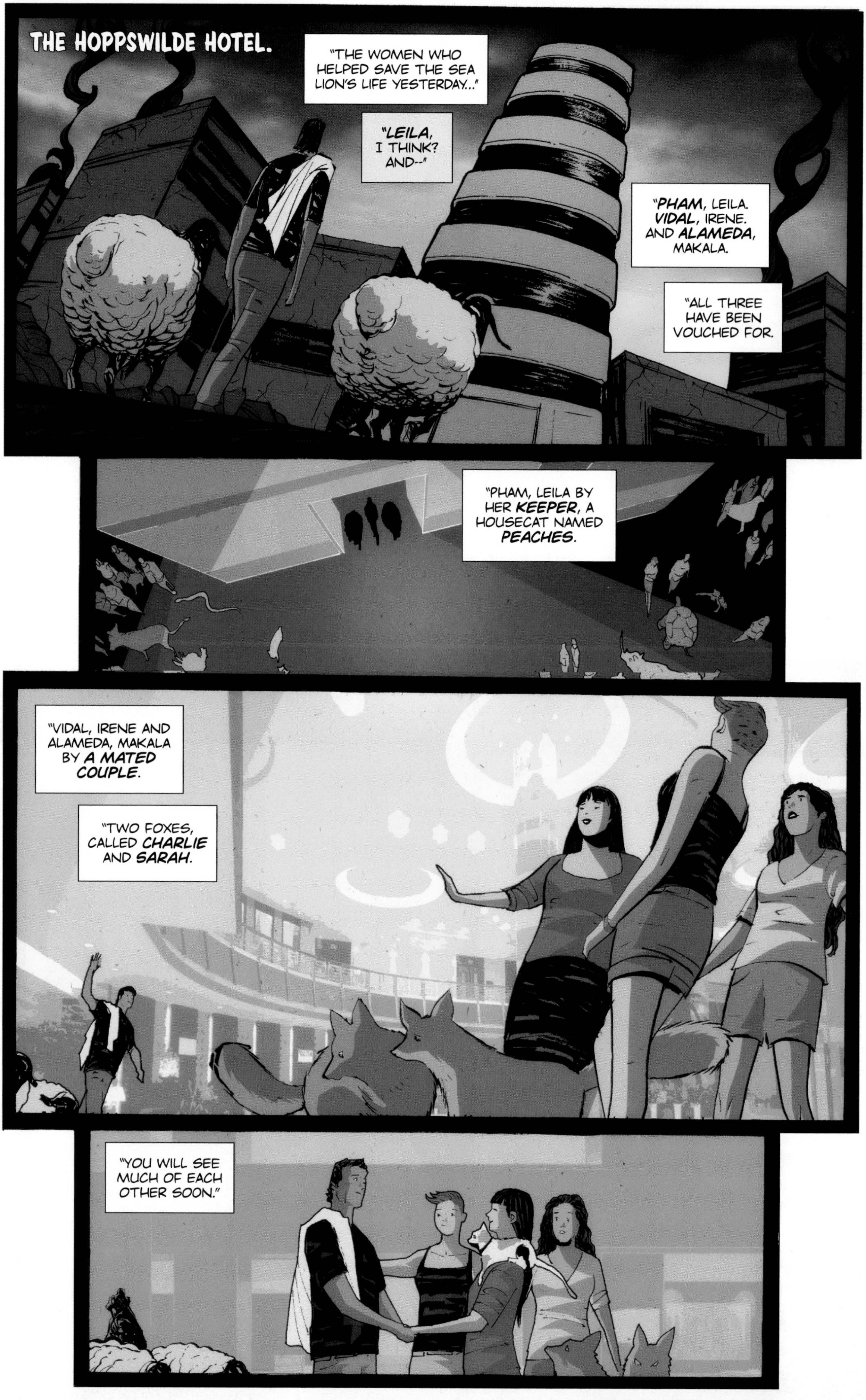
THE HOPPSWILDE HOTEL.
"THE WOMEN WHO HELPED SAVE THE SEA LION'S LIFE YESTERDAY..."
"LEILA, I THINK? AND--"
"PHAM, LEILA. VIDAL, IRENE. AND ALAMEDA, MAKALA.
"ALL THREE HAVE BEEN VOUCHED FOR.
"PHAM, LEILA BY HER KEEPER, A HOUSECAT NAMED PEACHES.
"VIDAL, IRENE AND ALAMEDA, MAKALA BY A MATED COUPLE.
"TWO FOXES, CALLED CHARLIE AND SARAH.
"YOU WILL SEE MUCH OF EACH OTHER SOON."

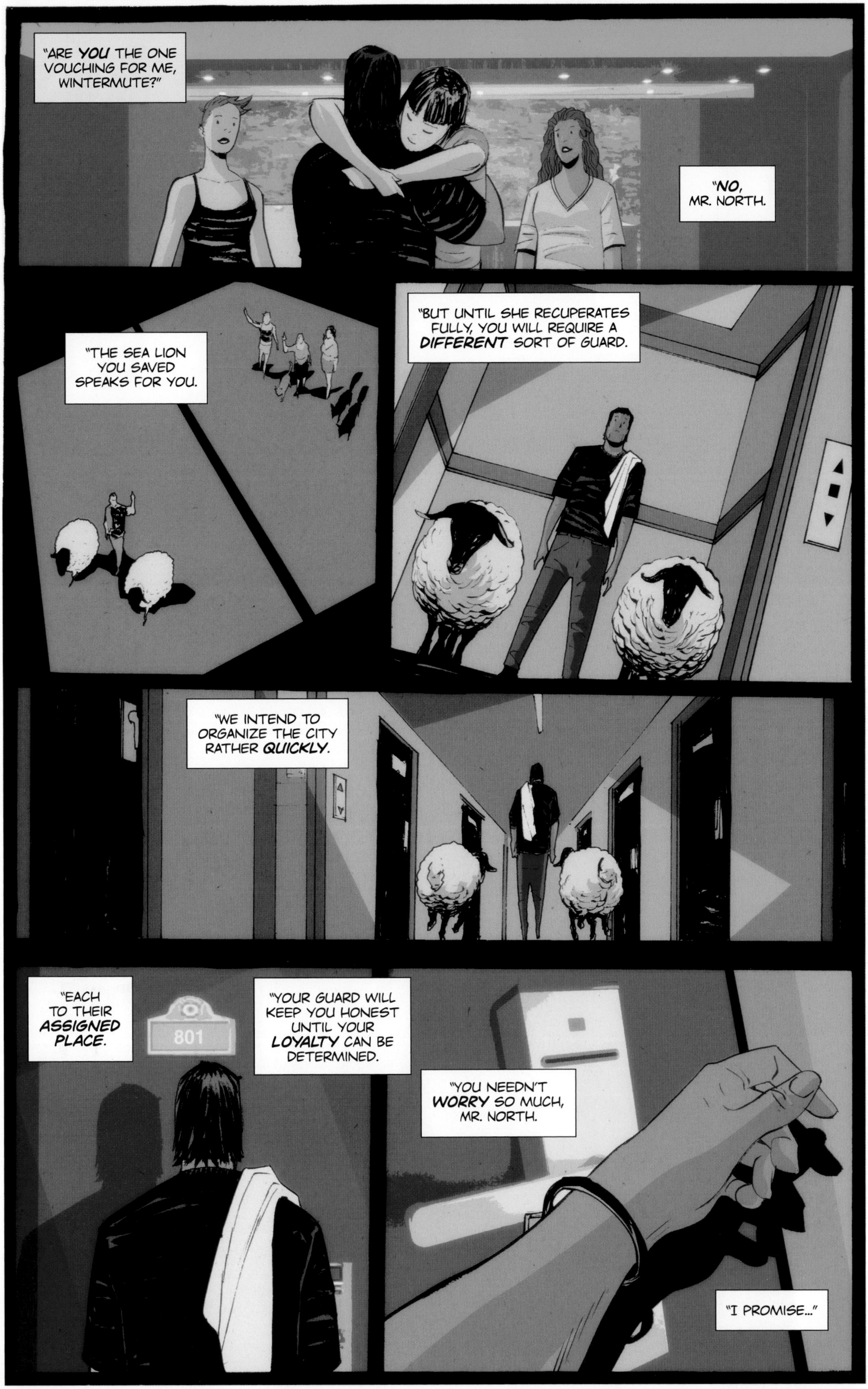
"ARE *YOU* THE ONE VOUCHING FOR ME, WINTERMUTE?"
"*NO*, MR. NORTH.
"THE SEA LION YOU SAVED SPEAKS FOR YOU.
"BUT UNTIL SHE RECUPERATES FULLY, YOU WILL REQUIRE A *DIFFERENT* SORT OF GUARD.
"WE INTEND TO ORGANIZE THE CITY RATHER *QUICKLY*.
"EACH TO THEIR *ASSIGNED PLACE*.
801
"YOUR GUARD WILL KEEP YOU HONEST UNTIL YOUR *LOYALTY* CAN BE DETERMINED.
"YOU NEEDN'T *WORRY* SO MUCH, MR. NORTH.
"I PROMISE..."

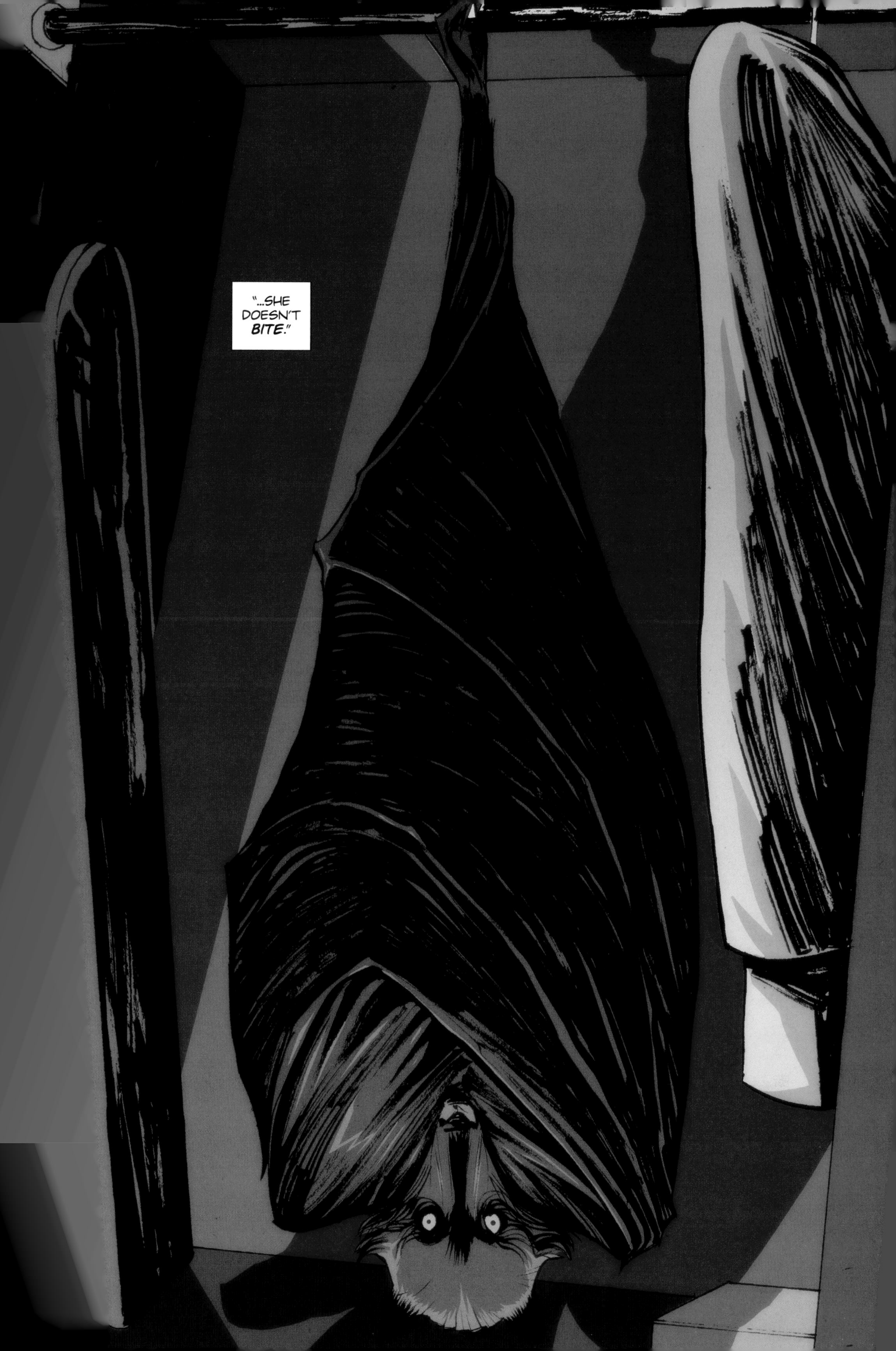
"...SHE DOESN'T BITE."

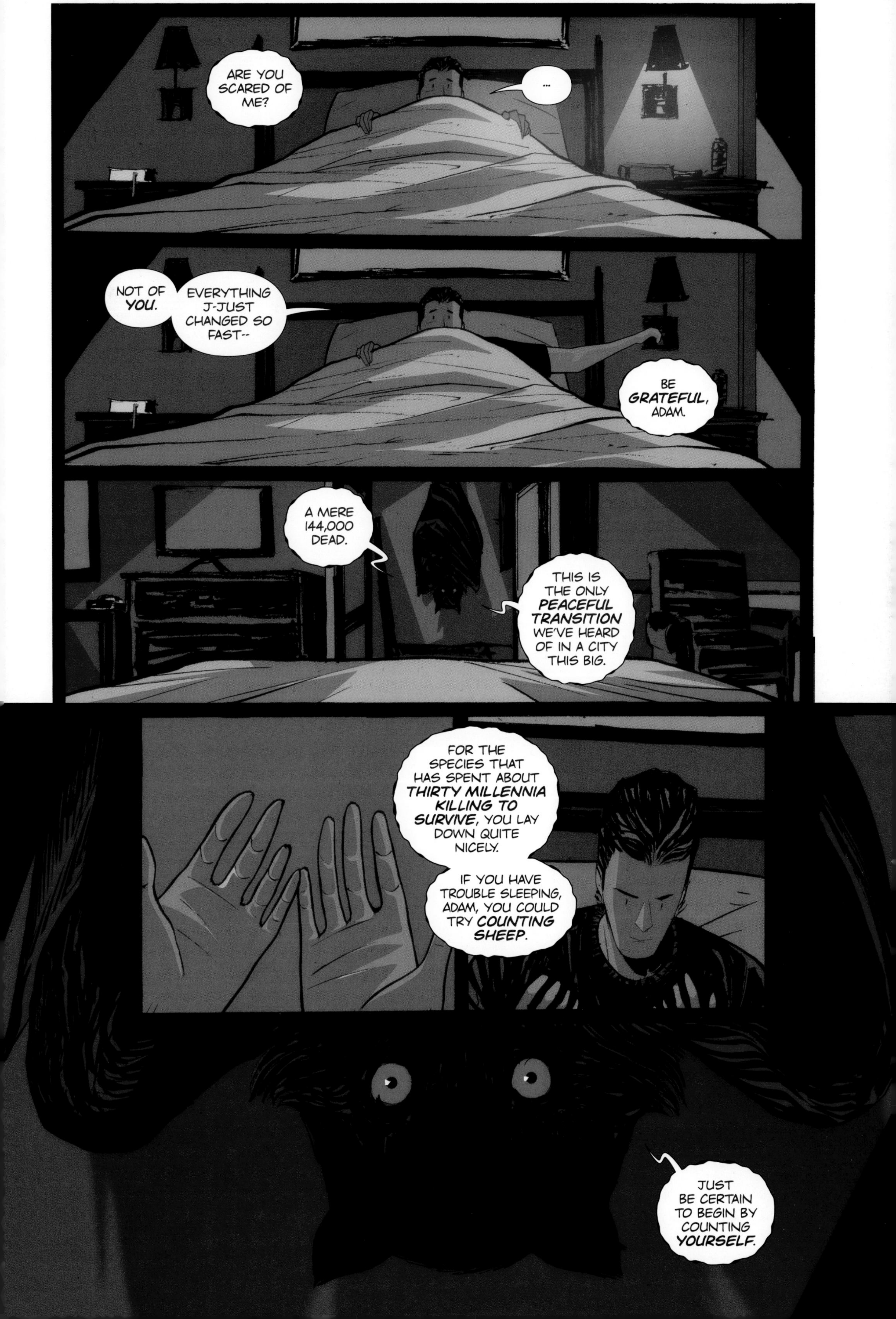

ARE YOU SCARED OF ME?
...
NOT OF YOU.
EVERYTHING J-JUST CHANGED SO FAST--
BE GRATEFUL, ADAM.
A MERE 144,000 DEAD.
THIS IS THE ONLY PEACEFUL TRANSITION WE'VE HEARD OF IN A CITY THIS BIG.
FOR THE SPECIES THAT HAS SPENT ABOUT THIRTY MILLENNIA KILLING TO SURVIVE, YOU LAY DOWN QUITE NICELY.
IF YOU HAVE TROUBLE SLEEPING, ADAM, YOU COULD TRY COUNTING SHEEP.
JUST BE CERTAIN TO BEGIN BY COUNTING YOURSELF.

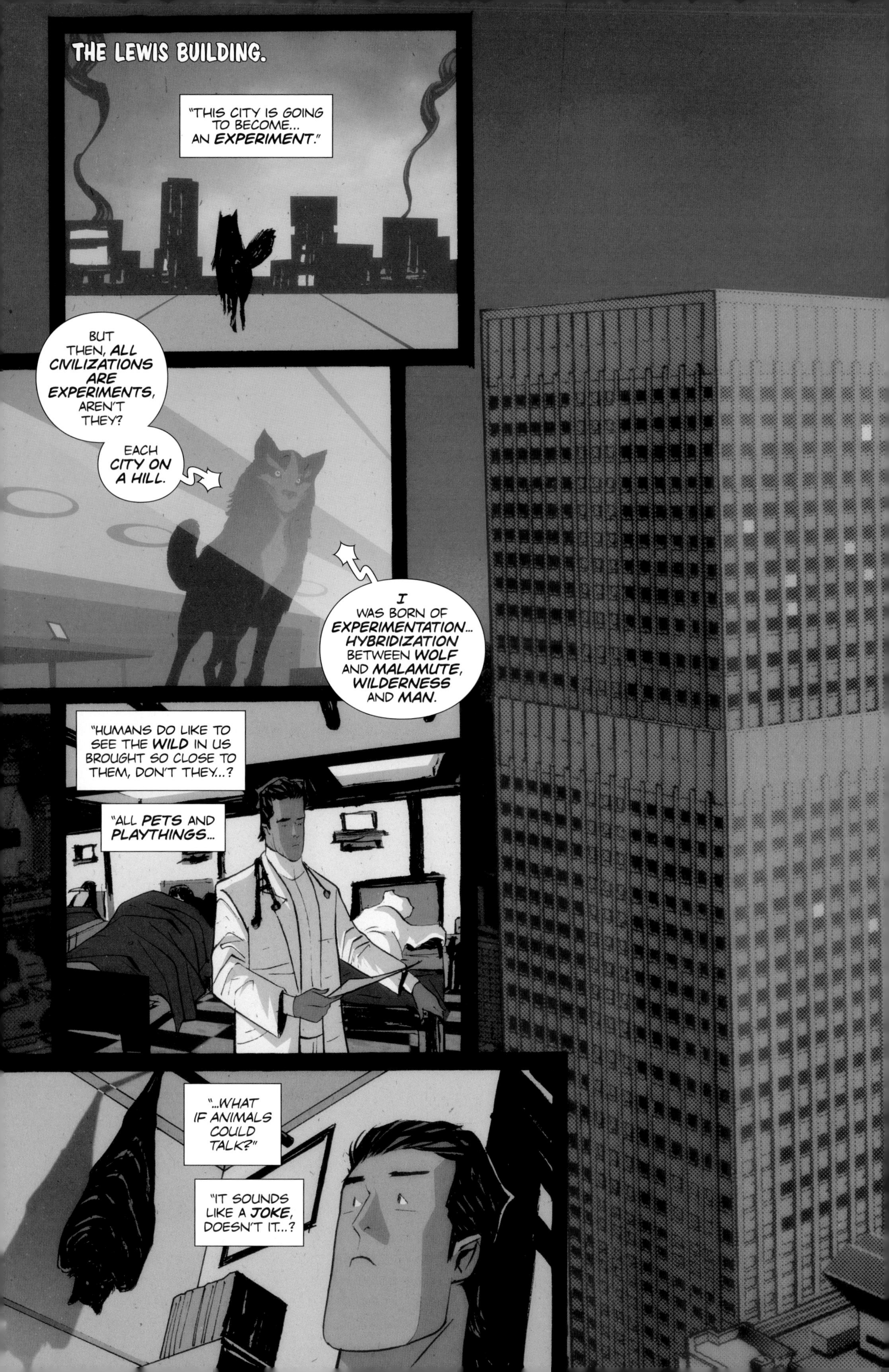
THE LEWIS BUILDING.
"THIS CITY IS GOING TO BECOME... AN EXPERIMENT."
BUT THEN, ALL CIVILIZATIONS ARE EXPERIMENTS, AREN'T THEY?
EACH CITY ON A HILL.
I WAS BORN OF EXPERIMENTATION... HYBRIDIZATION BETWEEN WOLF AND MALAMUTE, WILDERNESS AND MAN.
"HUMANS DO LIKE TO SEE THE WILD IN US BROUGHT SO CLOSE TO THEM, DON'T THEY...?
"ALL PETS AND PLAYTHINGS...
"...WHAT IF ANIMALS COULD TALK?"
"IT SOUNDS LIKE A JOKE, DOESN'T IT...?

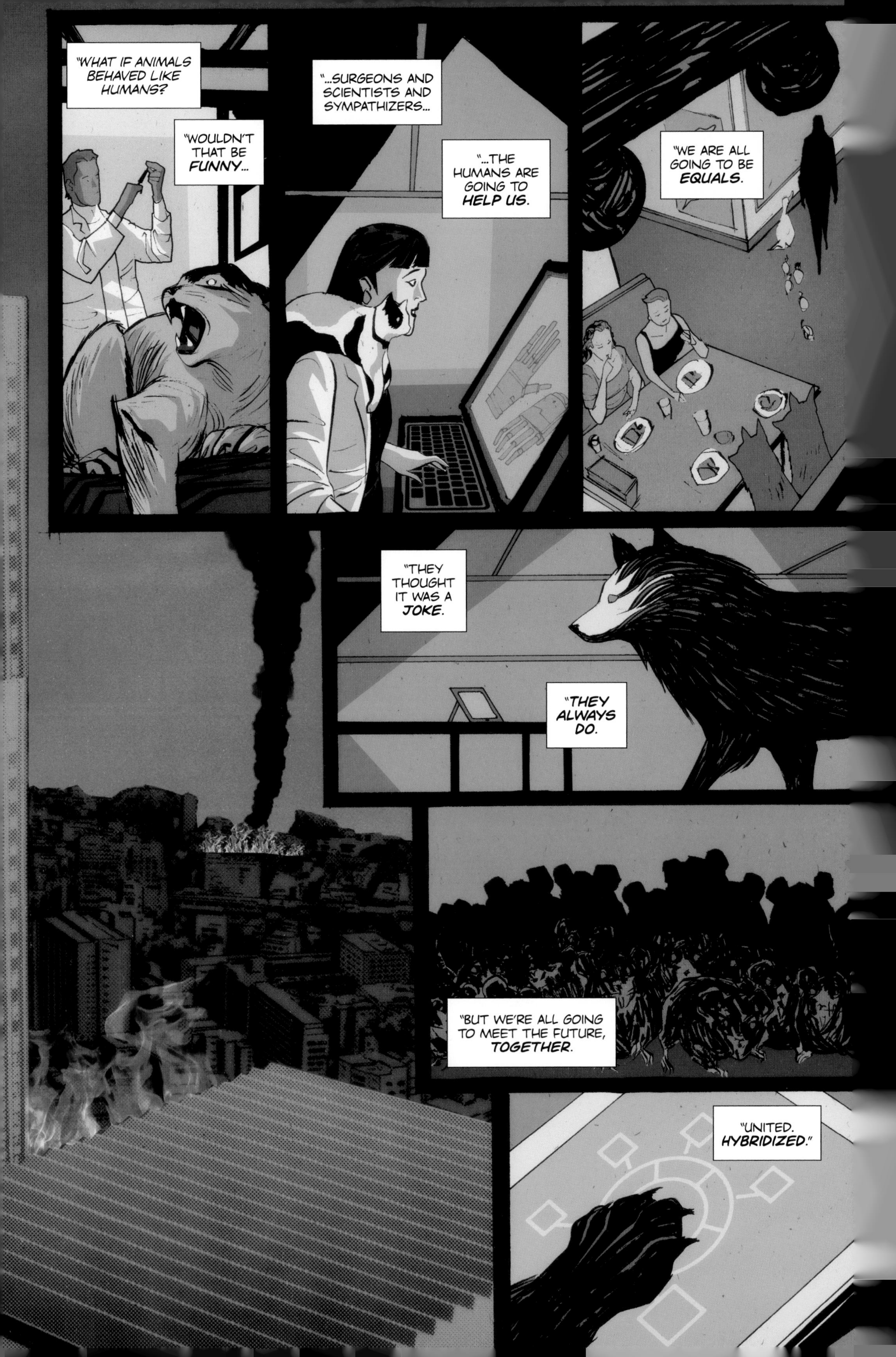
"WHAT IF ANIMALS BEHAVED LIKE HUMANS?
"WOULDN'T THAT BE FUNNY...
"...SURGEONS AND SCIENTISTS AND SYMPATHIZERS...
"...THE HUMANS ARE GOING TO HELP US.
"WE ARE ALL GOING TO BE EQUALS.
"THEY THOUGHT IT WAS A JOKE.
"THEY ALWAYS DO.
"BUT WE'RE ALL GOING TO MEET THE FUTURE, TOGETHER.
"UNITED. HYBRIDIZED."

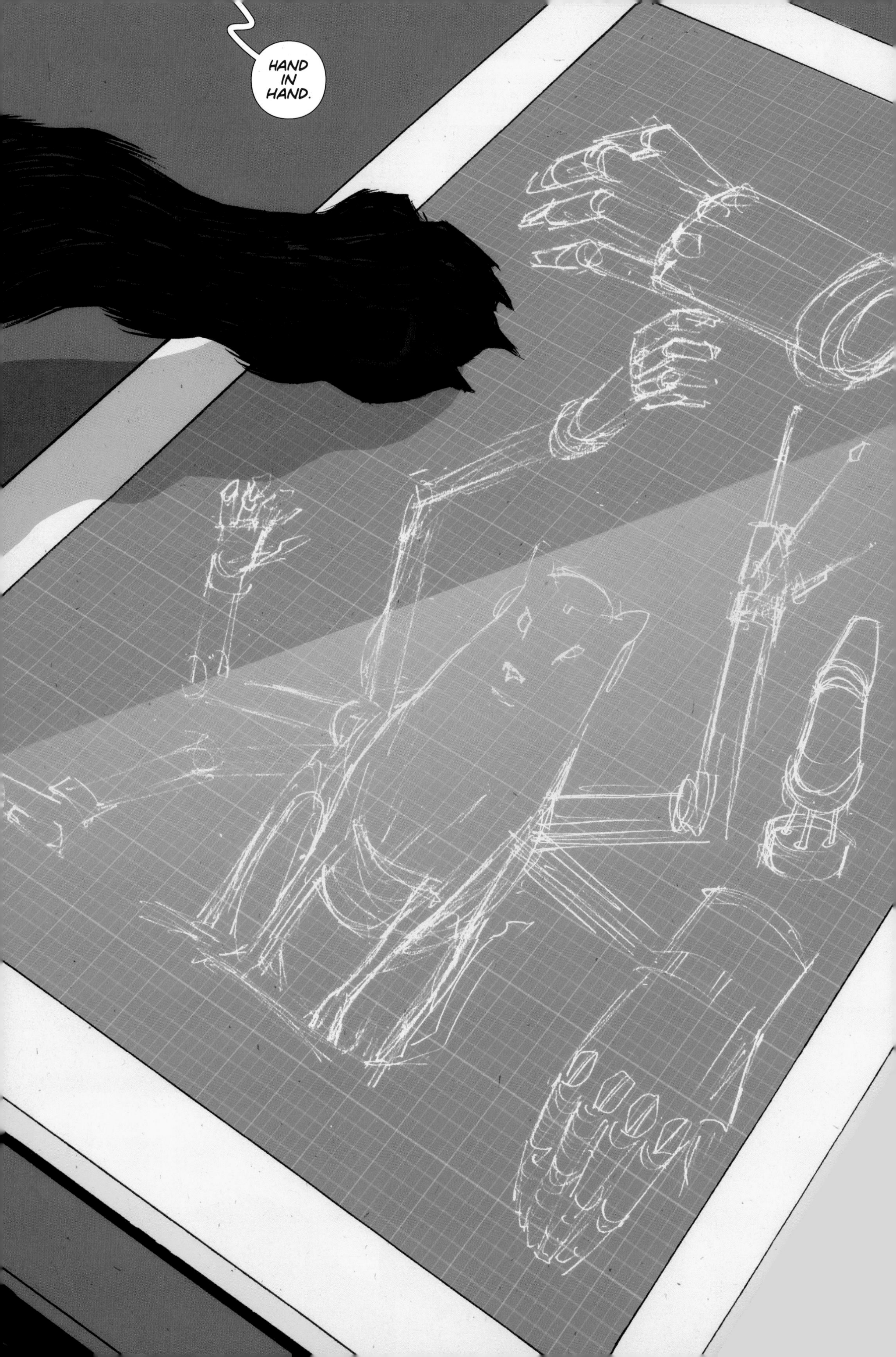
HAND IN HAND.

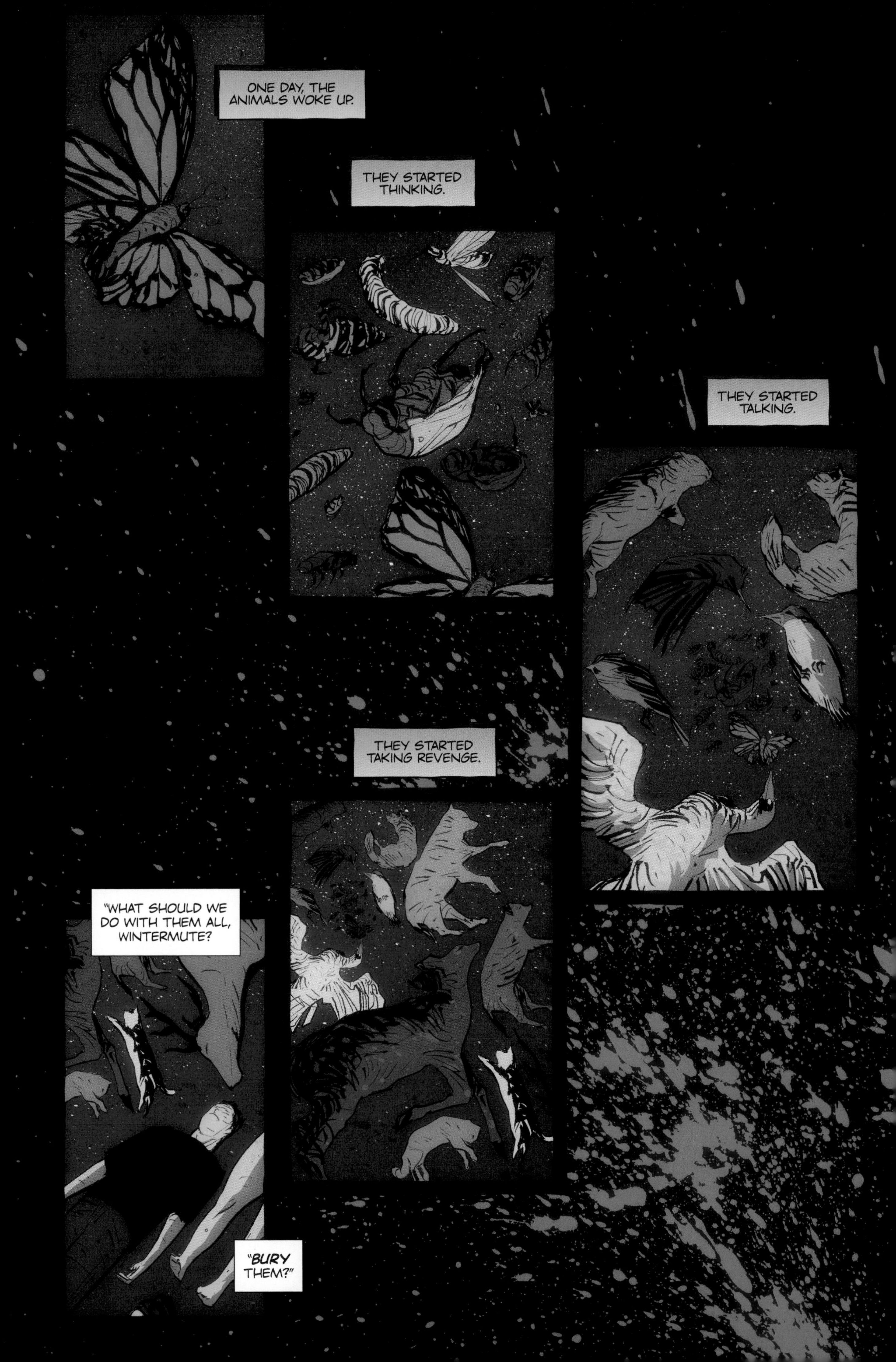
ONE DAY, THE ANIMALS WOKE UP.
THEY STARTED THINKING.
THEY STARTED TALKING.
THEY STARTED TAKING REVENGE.
"WHAT SHOULD WE DO WITH THEM ALL, WINTERMUTE?
"BURY THEM?"

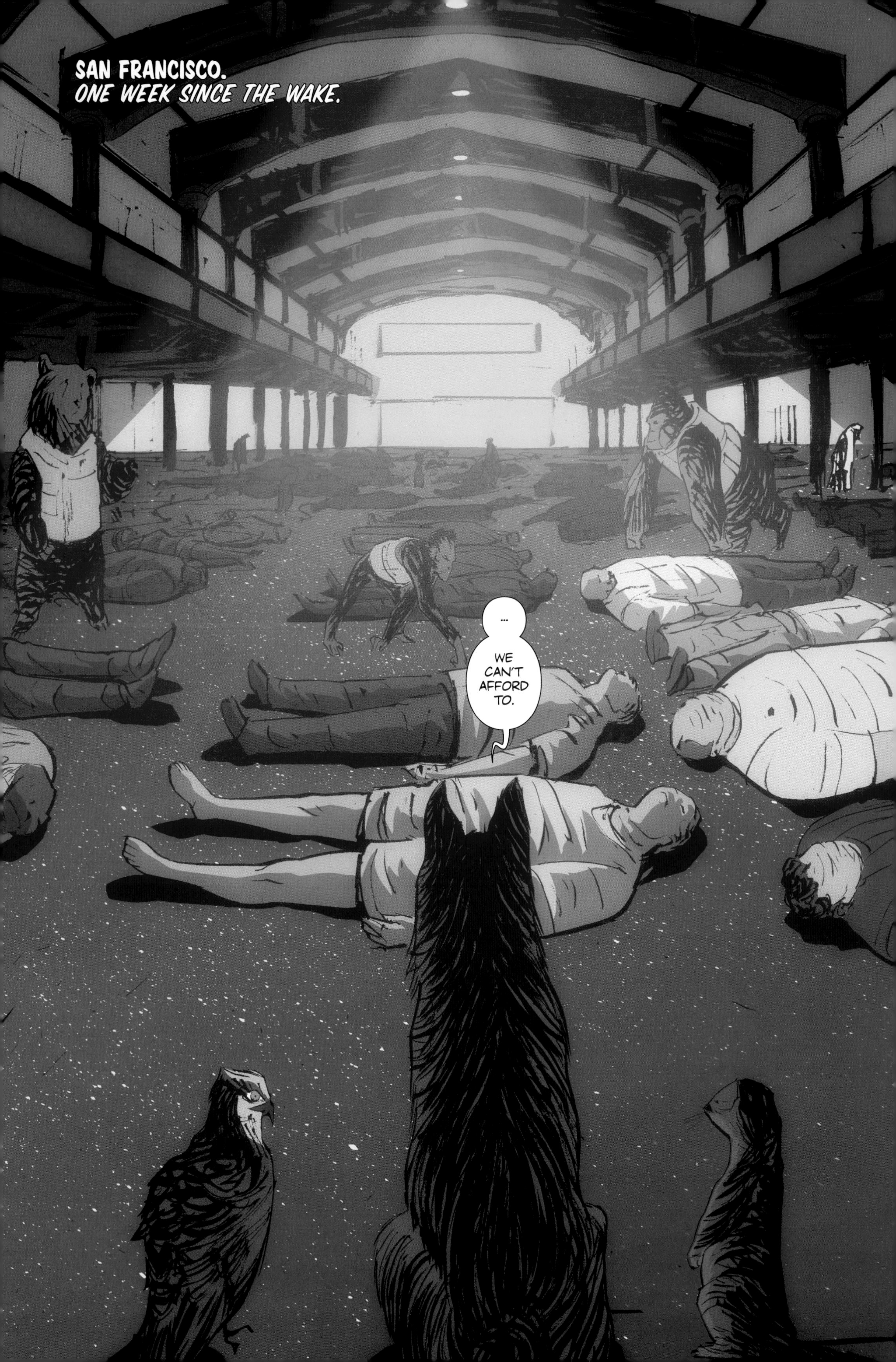
SAN FRANCISCO.
ONE WEEK SINCE THE WAKE.
...
WE CAN'T AFFORD TO.

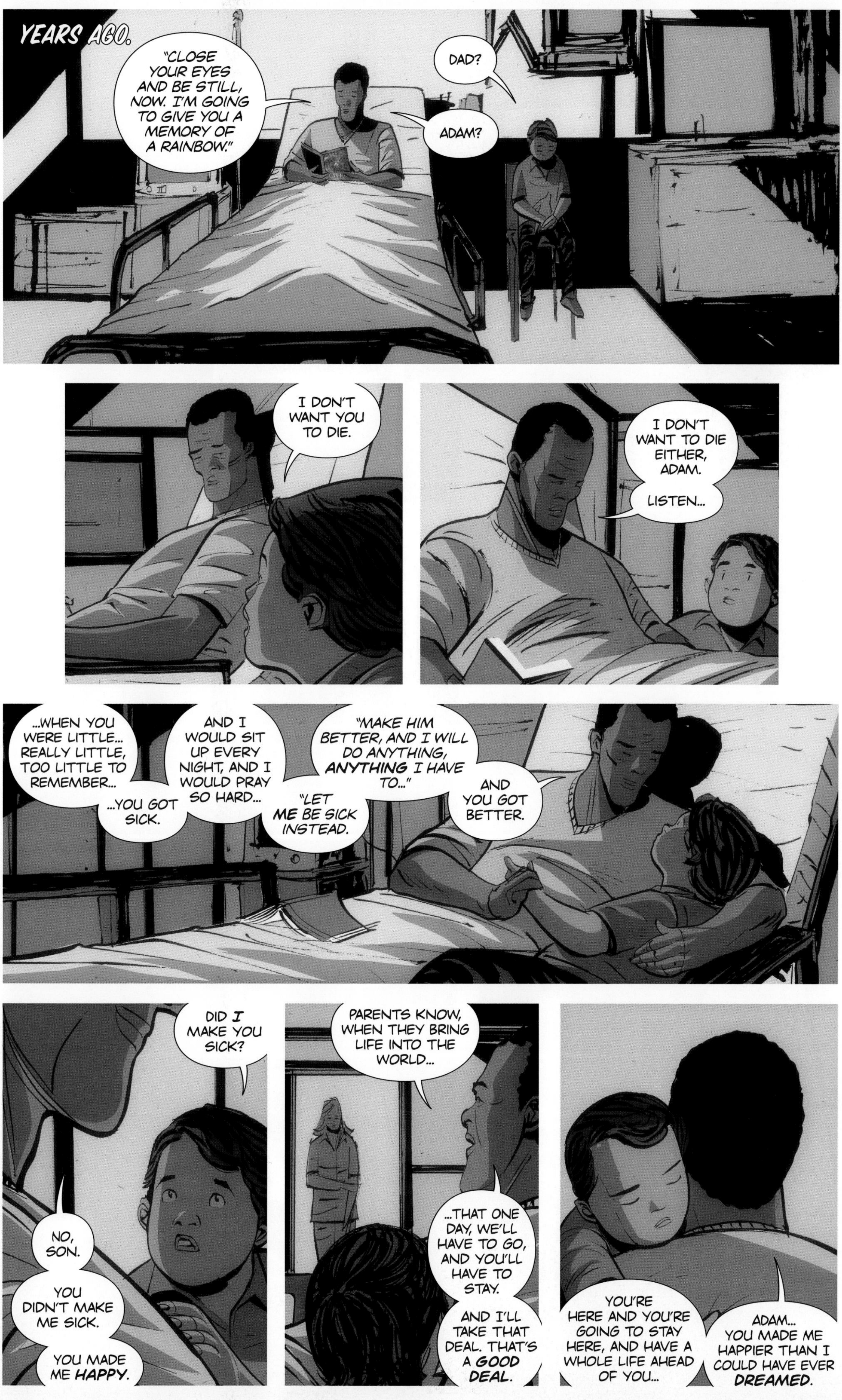
YEARS AGO.
"CLOSE YOUR EYES AND BE STILL, NOW. I'M GOING TO GIVE YOU A MEMORY OF A RAINBOW."
DAD?
ADAM?
I DON'T WANT YOU TO DIE.
I DON'T WANT TO DIE EITHER, ADAM.
LISTEN...
...WHEN YOU WERE LITTLE... REALLY LITTLE, TOO LITTLE TO REMEMBER...
...YOU GOT SICK.
AND I WOULD SIT UP EVERY NIGHT, AND I WOULD PRAY SO HARD...
"LET ME BE SICK INSTEAD.
"MAKE HIM BETTER, AND I WILL DO ANYTHING, ANYTHING I HAVE TO..."
AND YOU GOT BETTER.
DID I MAKE YOU SICK?
NO, SON.
YOU DIDN'T MAKE ME SICK.
YOU MADE ME HAPPY.
PARENTS KNOW, WHEN THEY BRING LIFE INTO THE WORLD...
...THAT ONE DAY, WE'LL HAVE TO GO, AND YOU'LL HAVE TO STAY.
AND I'LL TAKE THAT DEAL. THAT'S A GOOD DEAL.
YOU'RE HERE AND YOU'RE GOING TO STAY HERE, AND HAVE A WHOLE LIFE AHEAD OF YOU...
ADAM... YOU MADE ME HAPPIER THAN I COULD HAVE EVER DREAMED.

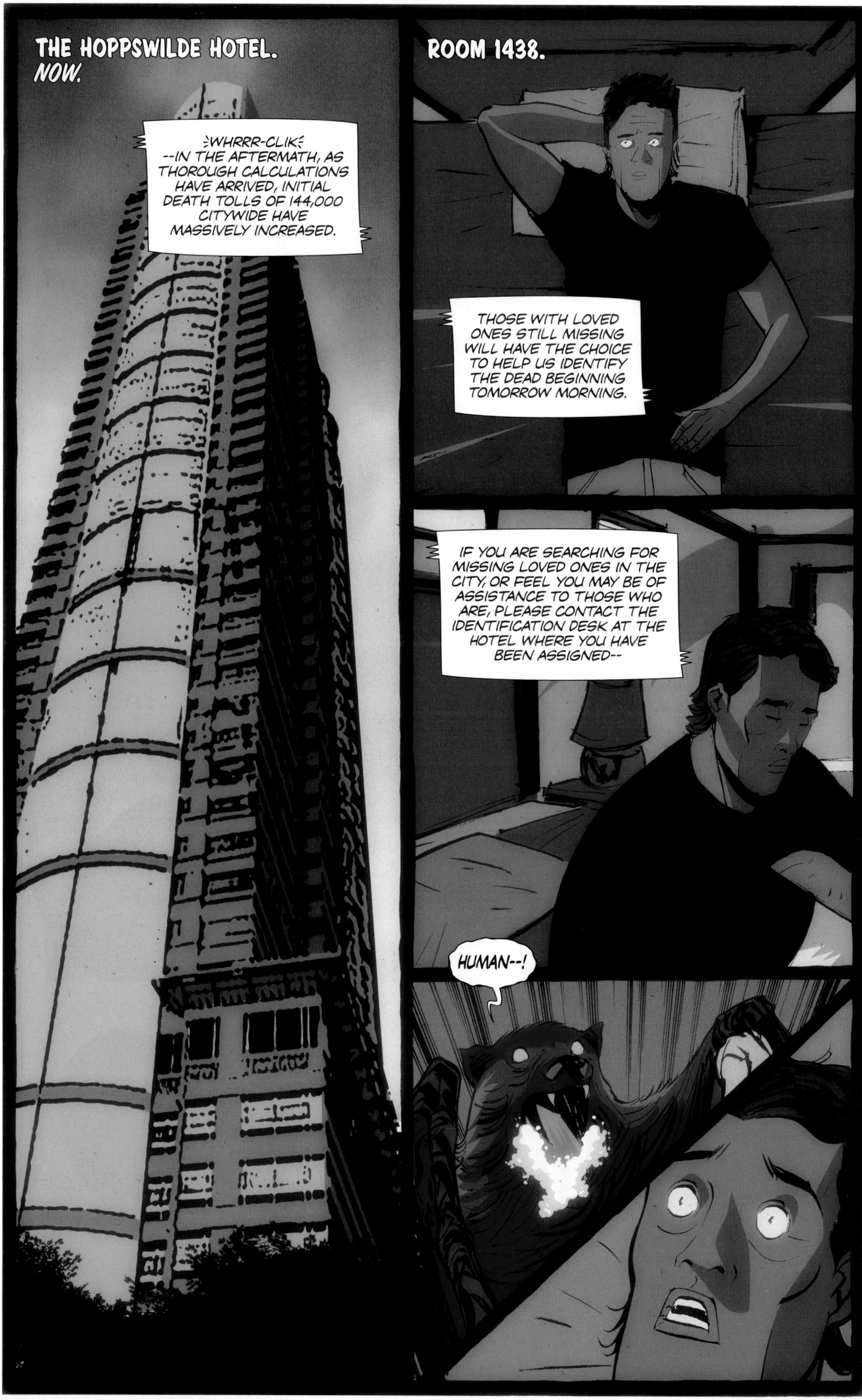
THE HOPPSWILDE HOTEL.
NOW.
WHRRR-CLIK --IN THE AFTERMATH, AS THOROUGH CALCULATIONS HAVE ARRIVED, INITIAL DEATH TOLLS OF 144,000 CITYWIDE HAVE MASSIVELY INCREASED.
ROOM 1438.
THOSE WITH LOVED ONES STILL MISSING WILL HAVE THE CHOICE TO HELP US IDENTIFY THE DEAD BEGINNING TOMORROW MORNING.
IF YOU ARE SEARCHING FOR MISSING LOVED ONES IN THE CITY, OR FEEL YOU MAY BE OF ASSISTANCE TO THOSE WHO ARE, PLEASE CONTACT THE IDENTIFICATION DESK AT THE HOTEL WHERE YOU HAVE BEEN ASSIGNED--
HUMAN--!

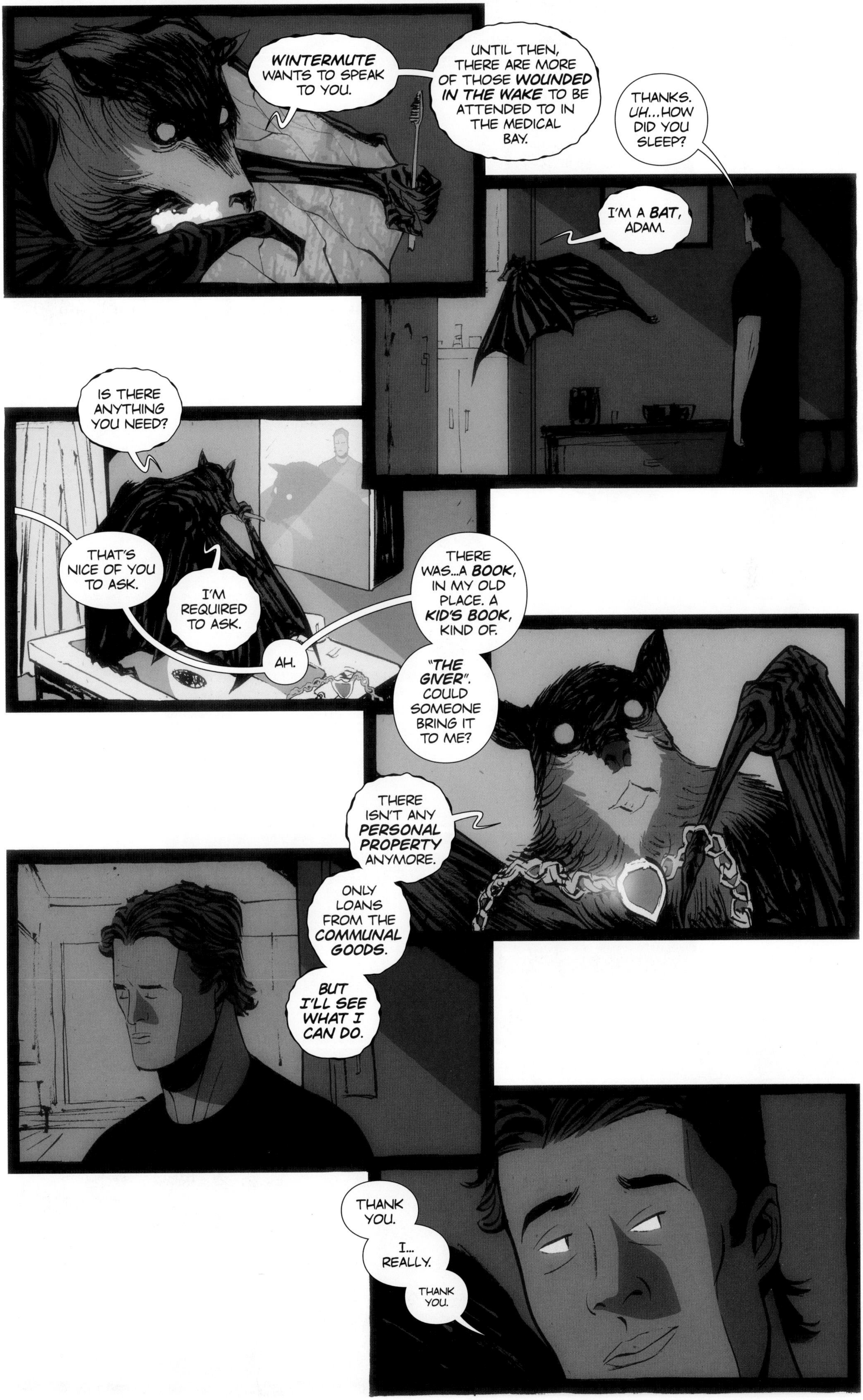
WINTERMUTE WANTS TO SPEAK TO YOU.
UNTIL THEN, THERE ARE MORE OF THOSE WOUNDED IN THE WAKE TO BE ATTENDED TO IN THE MEDICAL BAY.
THANKS. UH...HOW DID YOU SLEEP?
I'M A BAT, ADAM.
IS THERE ANYTHING YOU NEED?
THAT'S NICE OF YOU TO ASK.
I'M REQUIRED TO ASK.
AH.
THERE WAS...A BOOK, IN MY OLD PLACE. A KID'S BOOK, KIND OF.
"THE GIVER". COULD SOMEONE BRING IT TO ME?
THERE ISN'T ANY PERSONAL PROPERTY ANYMORE.
ONLY LOANS FROM THE COMMUNAL GOODS.
BUT I'LL SEE WHAT I CAN DO.
THANK YOU.
I... REALLY.
THANK YOU.

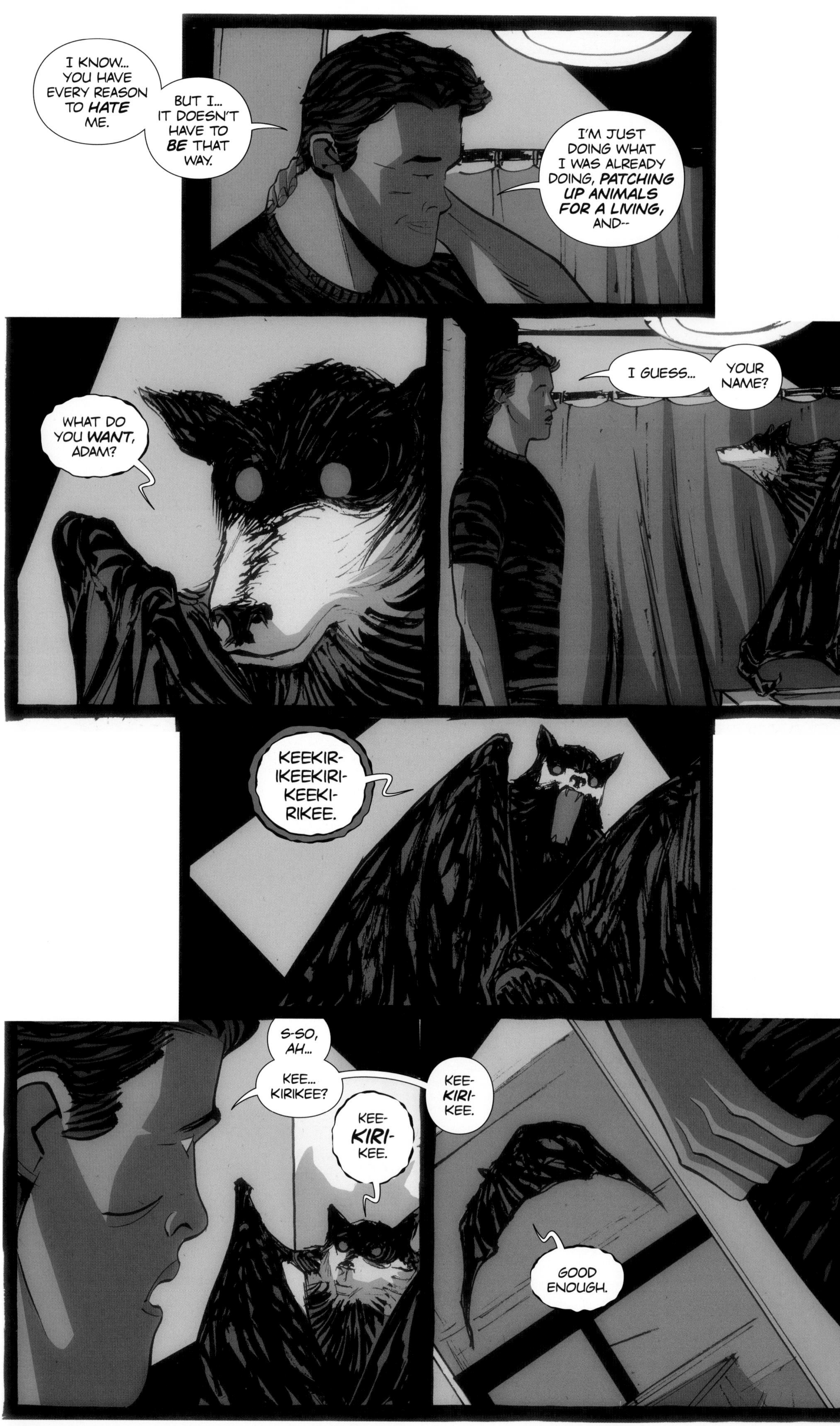
I KNOW... YOU HAVE EVERY REASON TO HATE ME.
BUT I... IT DOESN'T HAVE TO BE THAT WAY.
I'M JUST DOING WHAT I WAS ALREADY DOING, PATCHING UP ANIMALS FOR A LIVING, AND--
WHAT DO YOU WANT, ADAM?
I GUESS...
YOUR NAME?
KEEKIR-IKEEKIRI-KEEKI-RIKEE.
S-SO, AH...
KEE... KIRIKEE?
KEE-KIRI-KEE.
KEE-KIRI-KEE.
GOOD ENOUGH.

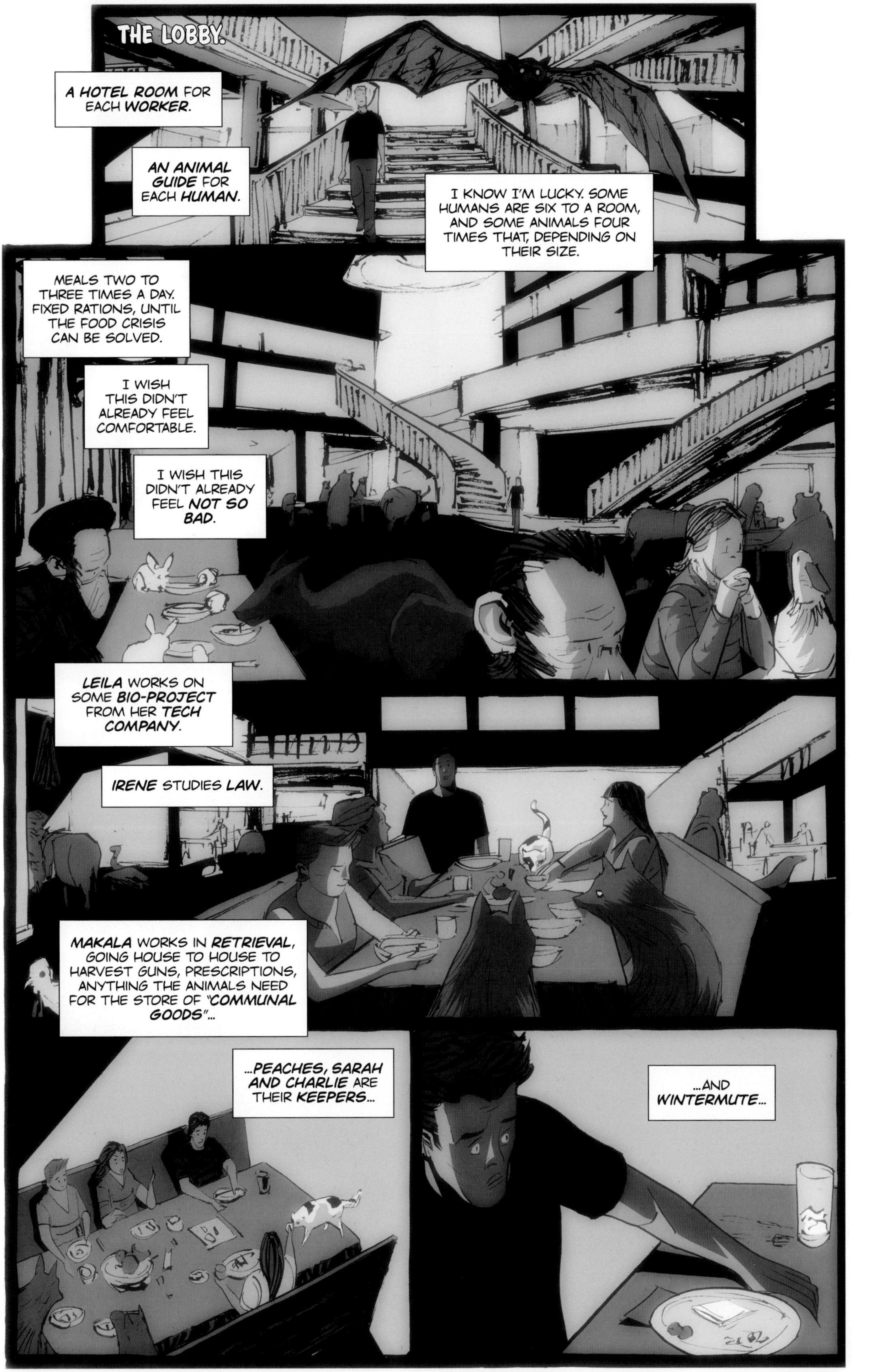
THE LOBBY.
A HOTEL ROOM FOR EACH WORKER.
AN ANIMAL GUIDE FOR EACH HUMAN.
I KNOW I'M LUCKY. SOME HUMANS ARE SIX TO A ROOM, AND SOME ANIMALS FOUR TIMES THAT, DEPENDING ON THEIR SIZE.
MEALS TWO TO THREE TIMES A DAY. FIXED RATIONS, UNTIL THE FOOD CRISIS CAN BE SOLVED.
I WISH THIS DIDN'T ALREADY FEEL COMFORTABLE.
I WISH THIS DIDN'T ALREADY FEEL NOT SO BAD.
LEILA WORKS ON SOME BIO-PROJECT FROM HER TECH COMPANY.
IRENE STUDIES LAW.
MAKALA WORKS IN RETRIEVAL, GOING HOUSE TO HOUSE TO HARVEST GUNS, PRESCRIPTIONS, ANYTHING THE ANIMALS NEED FOR THE STORE OF "COMMUNAL GOODS"...
...PEACHES, SARAH AND CHARLIE ARE THEIR KEEPERS...
...AND WINTERMUTE...

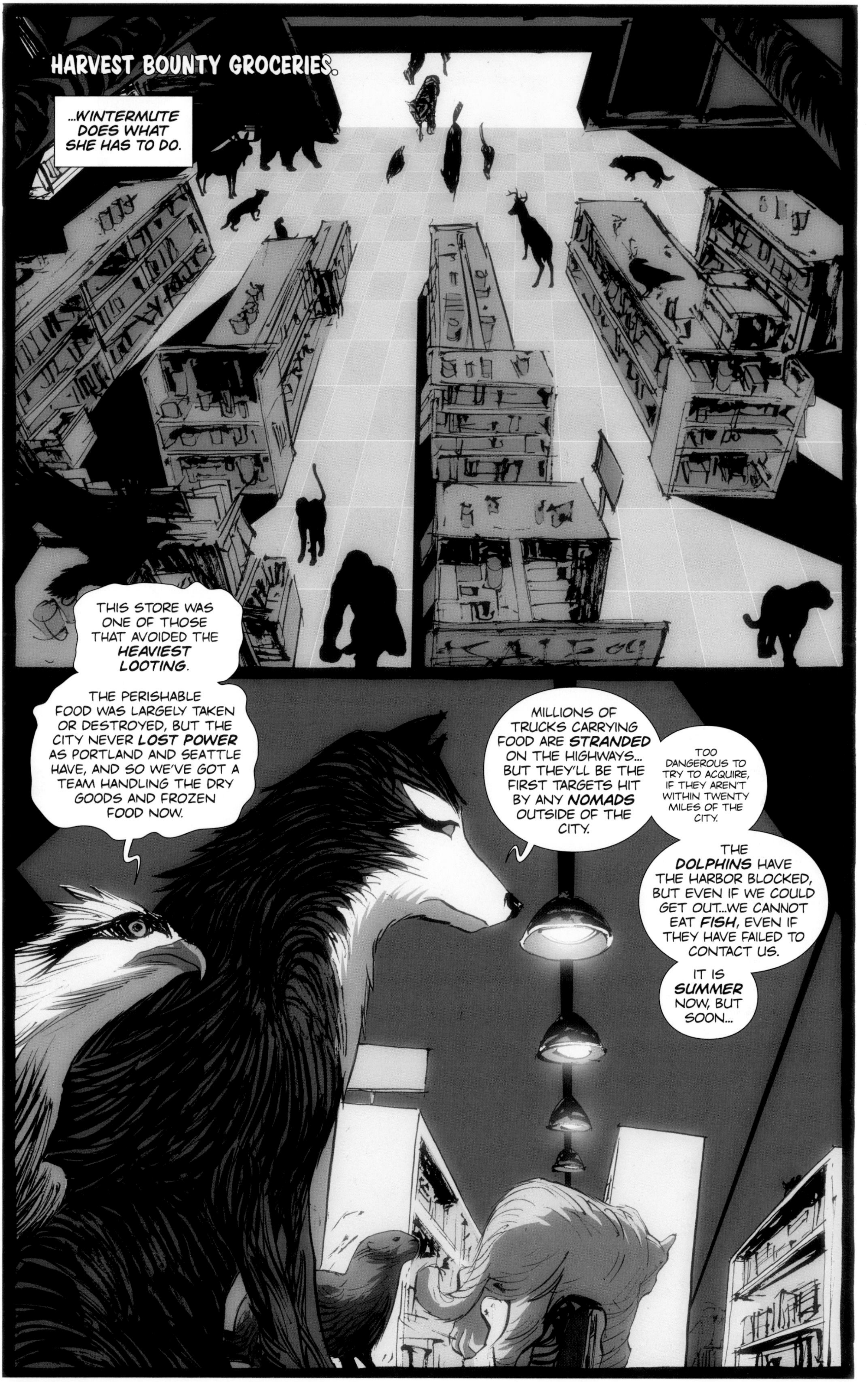

HARVEST BOUNTY GROCERIES.
...WINTERMUTE DOES WHAT SHE HAS TO DO.
THIS STORE WAS ONE OF THOSE THAT AVOIDED THE HEAVIEST LOOTING.
THE PERISHABLE FOOD WAS LARGELY TAKEN OR DESTROYED, BUT THE CITY NEVER LOST POWER AS PORTLAND AND SEATTLE HAVE, AND SO WE'VE GOT A TEAM HANDLING THE DRY GOODS AND FROZEN FOOD NOW.
MILLIONS OF TRUCKS CARRYING FOOD ARE STRANDED ON THE HIGHWAYS... BUT THEY'LL BE THE FIRST TARGETS HIT BY ANY NOMADS OUTSIDE OF THE CITY.
TOO DANGEROUS TO TRY TO ACQUIRE, IF THEY AREN'T WITHIN TWENTY MILES OF THE CITY.
THE DOLPHINS HAVE THE HARBOR BLOCKED, BUT EVEN IF WE COULD GET OUT...WE CANNOT EAT FISH, EVEN IF THEY HAVE FAILED TO CONTACT US.
IT IS SUMMER NOW, BUT SOON...

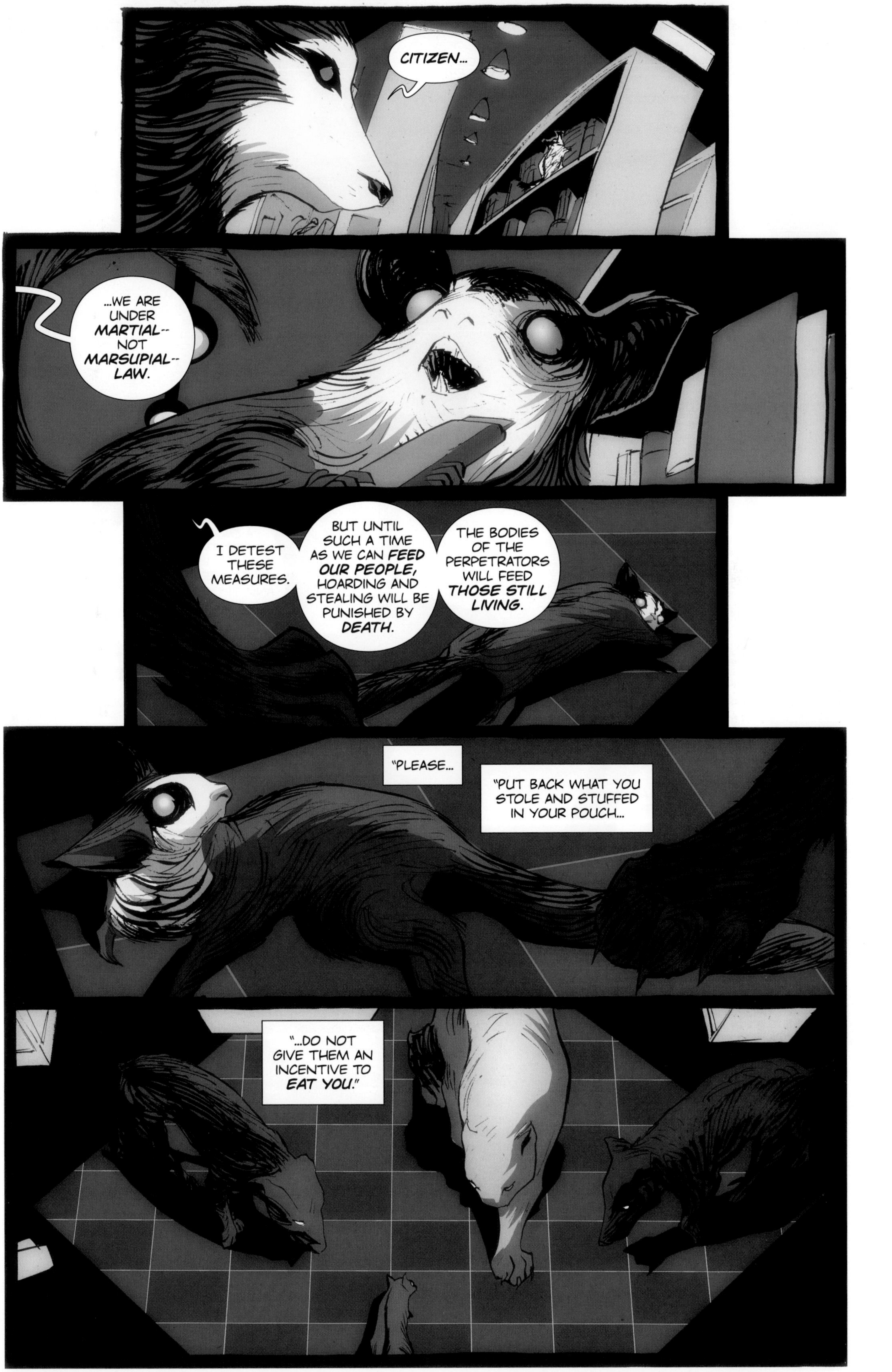
CITIZEN...
...WE ARE UNDER MARTIAL-- NOT MARSUPIAL-- LAW.
I DETEST THESE MEASURES.
BUT UNTIL SUCH A TIME AS WE CAN FEED OUR PEOPLE, HOARDING AND STEALING WILL BE PUNISHED BY DEATH.
THE BODIES OF THE PERPETRATORS WILL FEED THOSE STILL LIVING.
"PLEASE...
"PUT BACK WHAT YOU STOLE AND STUFFED IN YOUR POUCH...
"...DO NOT GIVE THEM AN INCENTIVE TO EAT YOU."

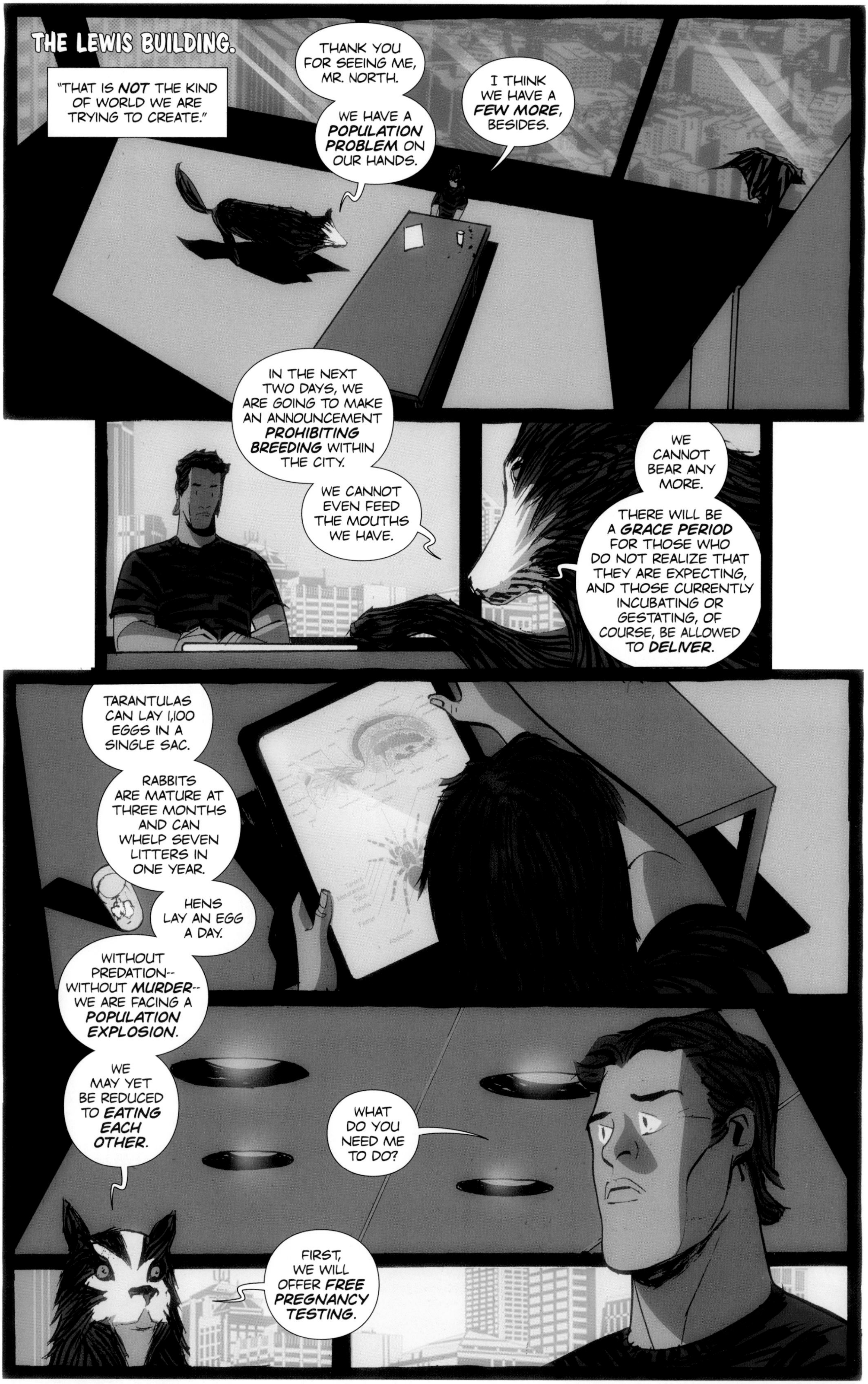
THE LEWIS BUILDING.
"THAT IS NOT THE KIND OF WORLD WE ARE TRYING TO CREATE."
THANK YOU FOR SEEING ME, MR. NORTH.
WE HAVE A POPULATION PROBLEM ON OUR HANDS.
I THINK WE HAVE A FEW MORE, BESIDES.
IN THE NEXT TWO DAYS, WE ARE GOING TO MAKE AN ANNOUNCEMENT PROHIBITING BREEDING WITHIN THE CITY.
WE CANNOT EVEN FEED THE MOUTHS WE HAVE.
WE CANNOT BEAR ANY MORE.
THERE WILL BE A GRACE PERIOD FOR THOSE WHO DO NOT REALIZE THAT THEY ARE EXPECTING, AND THOSE CURRENTLY INCUBATING OR GESTATING, OF COURSE, BE ALLOWED TO DELIVER.
TARANTULAS CAN LAY 1,100 EGGS IN A SINGLE SAC.
RABBITS ARE MATURE AT THREE MONTHS AND CAN WHELP SEVEN LITTERS IN ONE YEAR.
HENS LAY AN EGG A DAY.
WITHOUT PREDATION-- WITHOUT MURDER-- WE ARE FACING A POPULATION EXPLOSION.
WE MAY YET BE REDUCED TO EATING EACH OTHER.
WHAT DO YOU NEED ME TO DO?
FIRST, WE WILL OFFER FREE PREGNANCY TESTING.

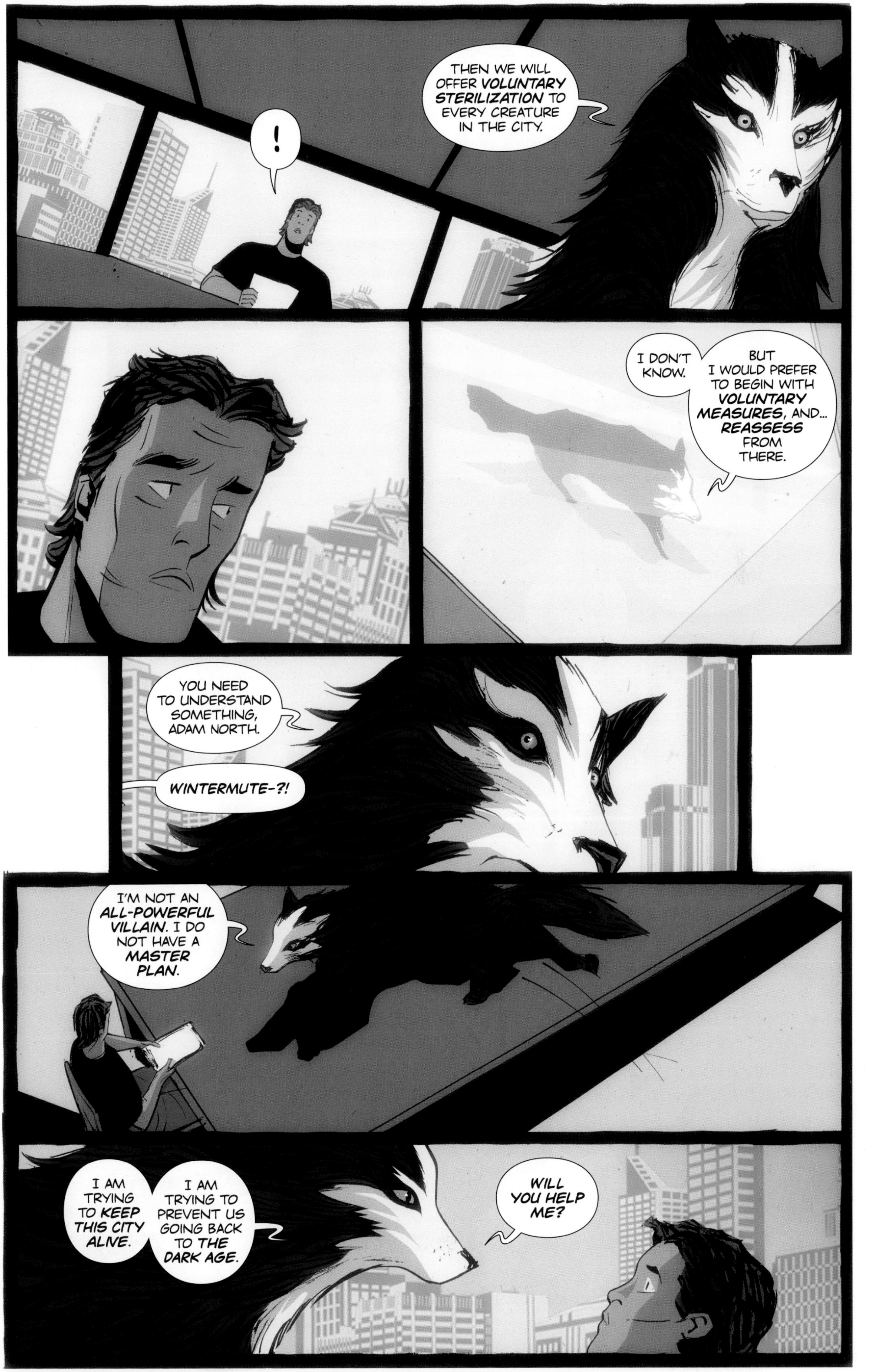
THEN WE WILL OFFER VOLUNTARY STERILIZATION TO EVERY CREATURE IN THE CITY.
!
I DON'T KNOW.
BUT I WOULD PREFER TO BEGIN WITH VOLUNTARY MEASURES, AND... REASSESS FROM THERE.
YOU NEED TO UNDERSTAND SOMETHING, ADAM NORTH.
WINTERMUTE-?!
I'M NOT AN ALL-POWERFUL VILLAIN. I DO NOT HAVE A MASTER PLAN.
I AM TRYING TO KEEP THIS CITY ALIVE.
I AM TRYING TO PREVENT US GOING BACK TO THE DARK AGE.
WILL YOU HELP ME?

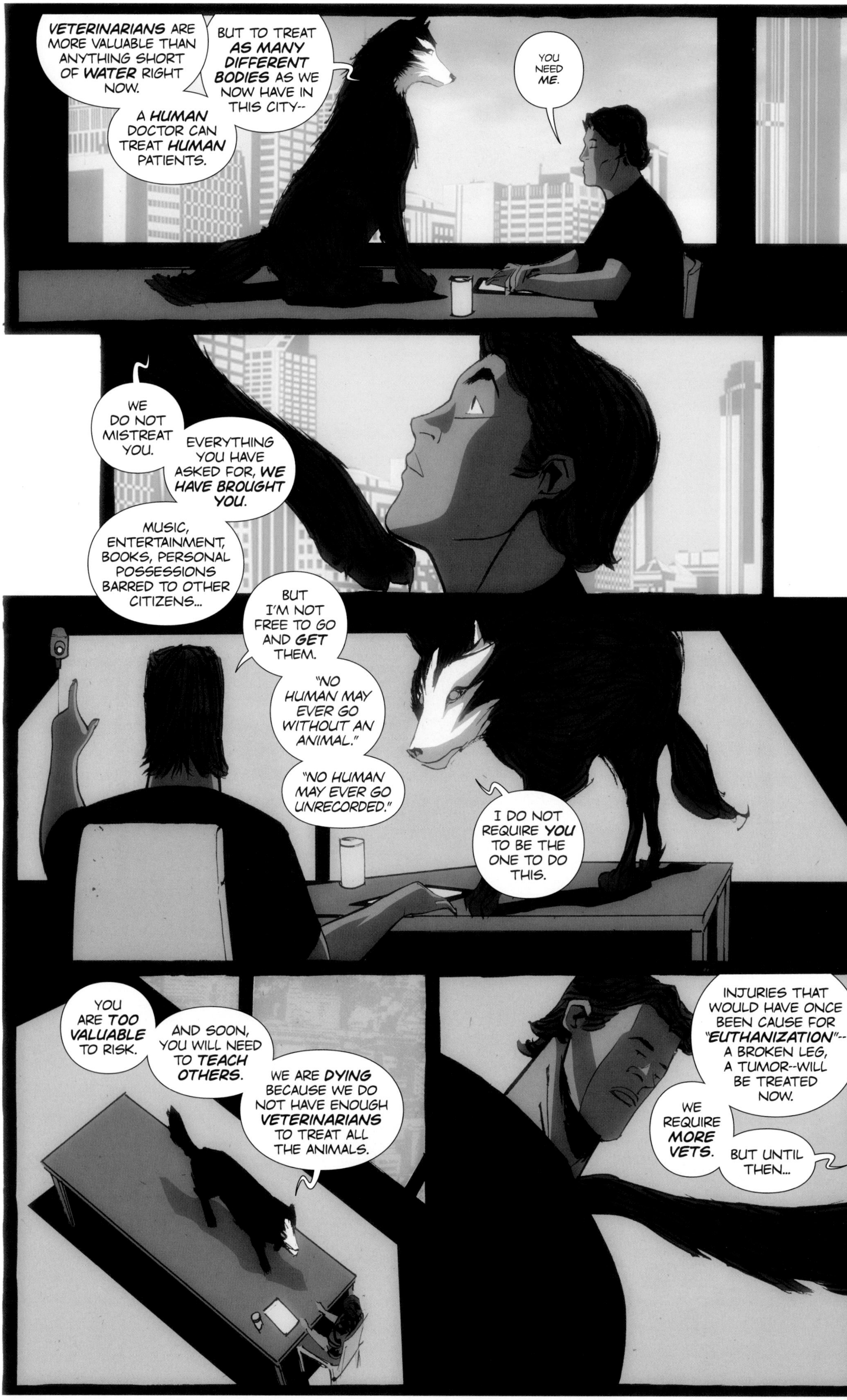
VETERINARIANS ARE MORE VALUABLE THAN ANYTHING SHORT OF WATER RIGHT NOW.
A HUMAN DOCTOR CAN TREAT HUMAN PATIENTS.
BUT TO TREAT AS MANY DIFFERENT BODIES AS WE NOW HAVE IN THIS CITY--
YOU NEED ME.
WE DO NOT MISTREAT YOU.
EVERYTHING YOU HAVE ASKED FOR, WE HAVE BROUGHT YOU.
MUSIC, ENTERTAINMENT, BOOKS, PERSONAL POSSESSIONS BARRED TO OTHER CITIZENS...
BUT I'M NOT FREE TO GO AND GET THEM.
"NO HUMAN MAY EVER GO WITHOUT AN ANIMAL."
"NO HUMAN MAY EVER GO UNRECORDED."
I DO NOT REQUIRE YOU TO BE THE ONE TO DO THIS.
YOU ARE TOO VALUABLE TO RISK.
AND SOON, YOU WILL NEED TO TEACH OTHERS.
WE ARE DYING BECAUSE WE DO NOT HAVE ENOUGH VETERINARIANS TO TREAT ALL THE ANIMALS.
INJURIES THAT WOULD HAVE ONCE BEEN CAUSE FOR "EUTHANIZATION"-- A BROKEN LEG, A TUMOR--WILL BE TREATED NOW.
WE REQUIRE MORE VETS.
BUT UNTIL THEN...

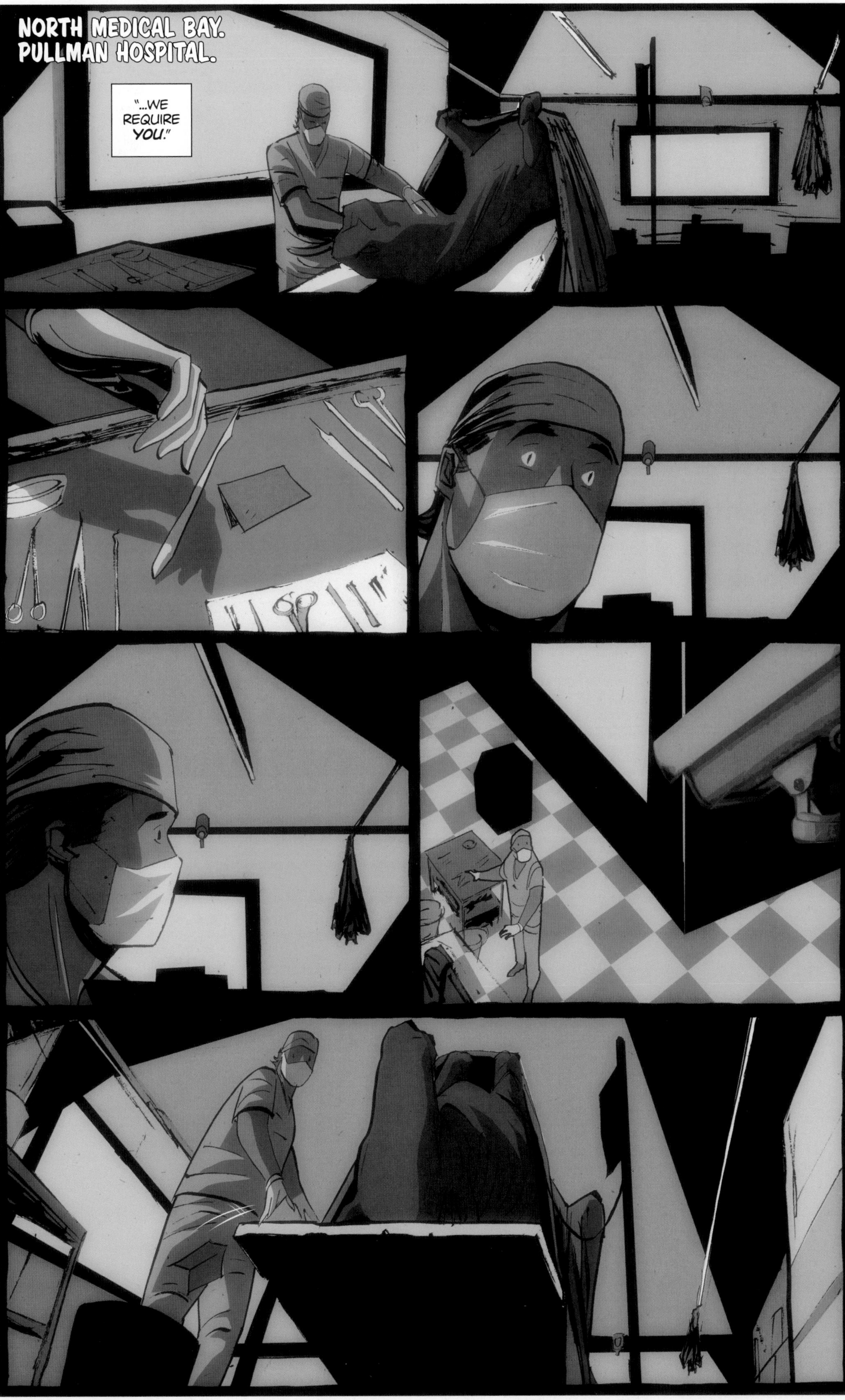
NORTH MEDICAL BAY.
PULLMAN HOSPITAL.
"...WE REQUIRE YOU."

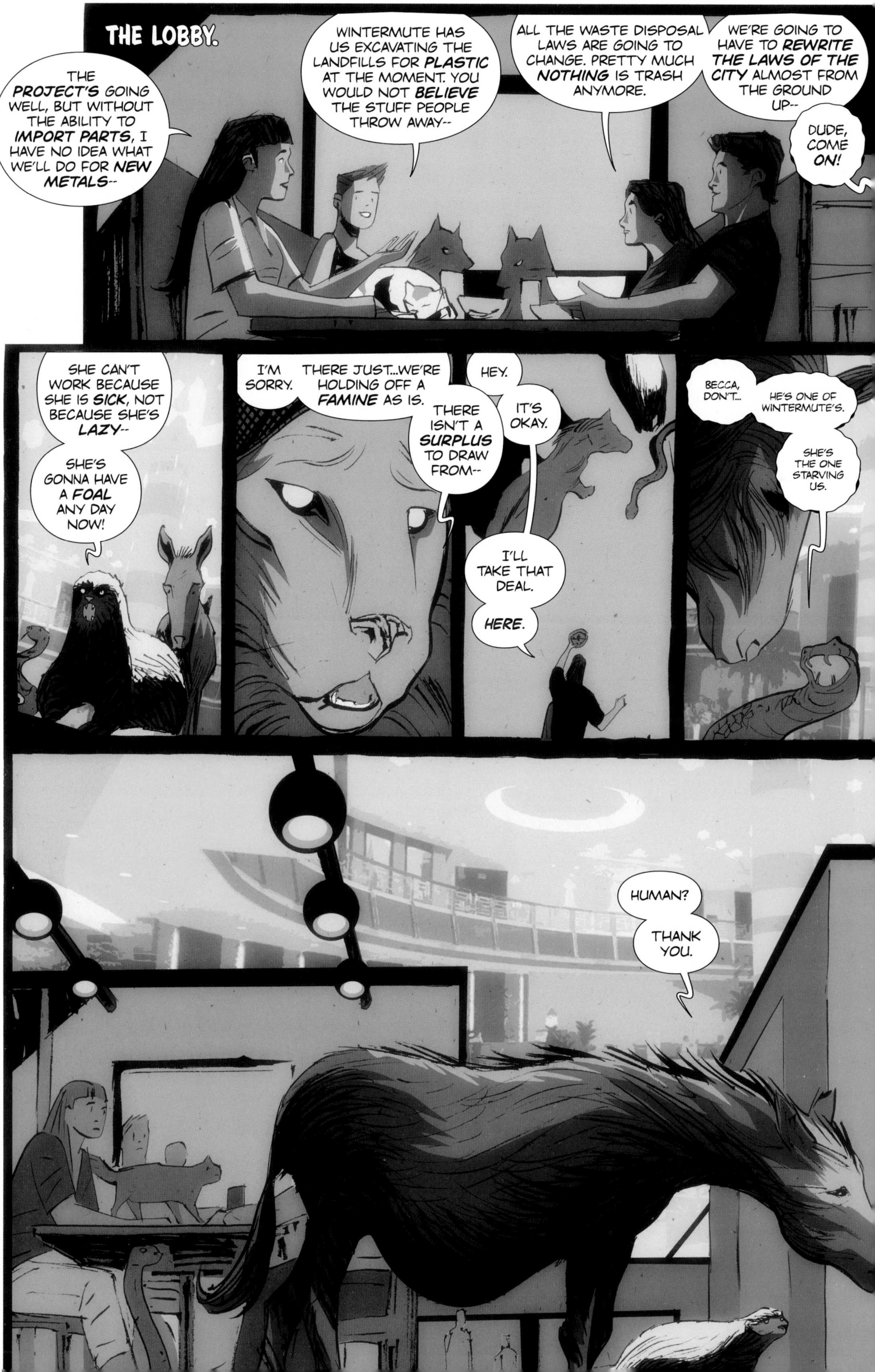
THE LOBBY.
THE PROJECT'S GOING WELL, BUT WITHOUT THE ABILITY TO IMPORT PARTS, I HAVE NO IDEA WHAT WE'LL DO FOR NEW METALS--
WINTERMUTE HAS US EXCAVATING THE LANDFILLS FOR PLASTIC AT THE MOMENT. YOU WOULD NOT BELIEVE THE STUFF PEOPLE THROW AWAY--
ALL THE WASTE DISPOSAL LAWS ARE GOING TO CHANGE. PRETTY MUCH NOTHING IS TRASH ANYMORE.
WE'RE GOING TO HAVE TO REWRITE THE LAWS OF THE CITY ALMOST FROM THE GROUND UP--
DUDE, COME ON!
SHE CAN'T WORK BECAUSE SHE IS SICK, NOT BECAUSE SHE'S LAZY--
SHE'S GONNA HAVE A FOAL ANY DAY NOW!
I'M SORRY.
THERE JUST...WE'RE HOLDING OFF A FAMINE AS IS.
THERE ISN'T A SURPLUS TO DRAW FROM--
HEY.
IT'S OKAY.
I'LL TAKE THAT DEAL.
HERE.
BECCA, DON'T...
HE'S ONE OF WINTERMUTE'S.
SHE'S THE ONE STARVING US.
HUMAN?
THANK YOU.

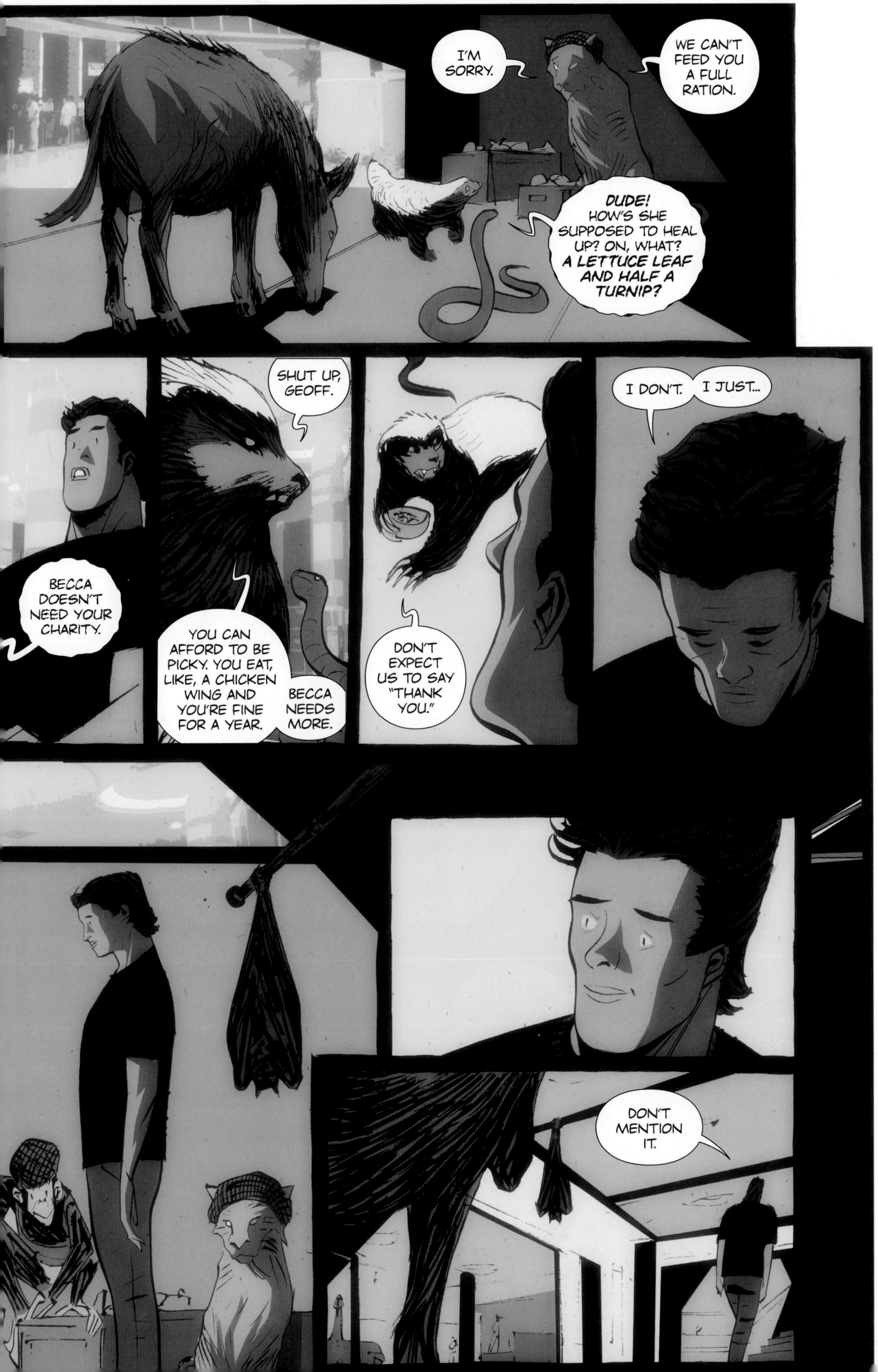
I'M SORRY.
WE CAN'T FEED YOU A FULL RATION.
DUDE! HOW'S SHE SUPPOSED TO HEAL UP? ON, WHAT? A LETTUCE LEAF AND HALF A TURNIP?
SHUT UP, GEOFF.
BECCA DOESN'T NEED YOUR CHARITY.
YOU CAN AFFORD TO BE PICKY. YOU EAT, LIKE, A CHICKEN WING AND YOU'RE FINE FOR A YEAR.
BECCA NEEDS MORE.
DON'T EXPECT US TO SAY "THANK YOU."
I DON'T.
I JUST...
DON'T MENTION IT.

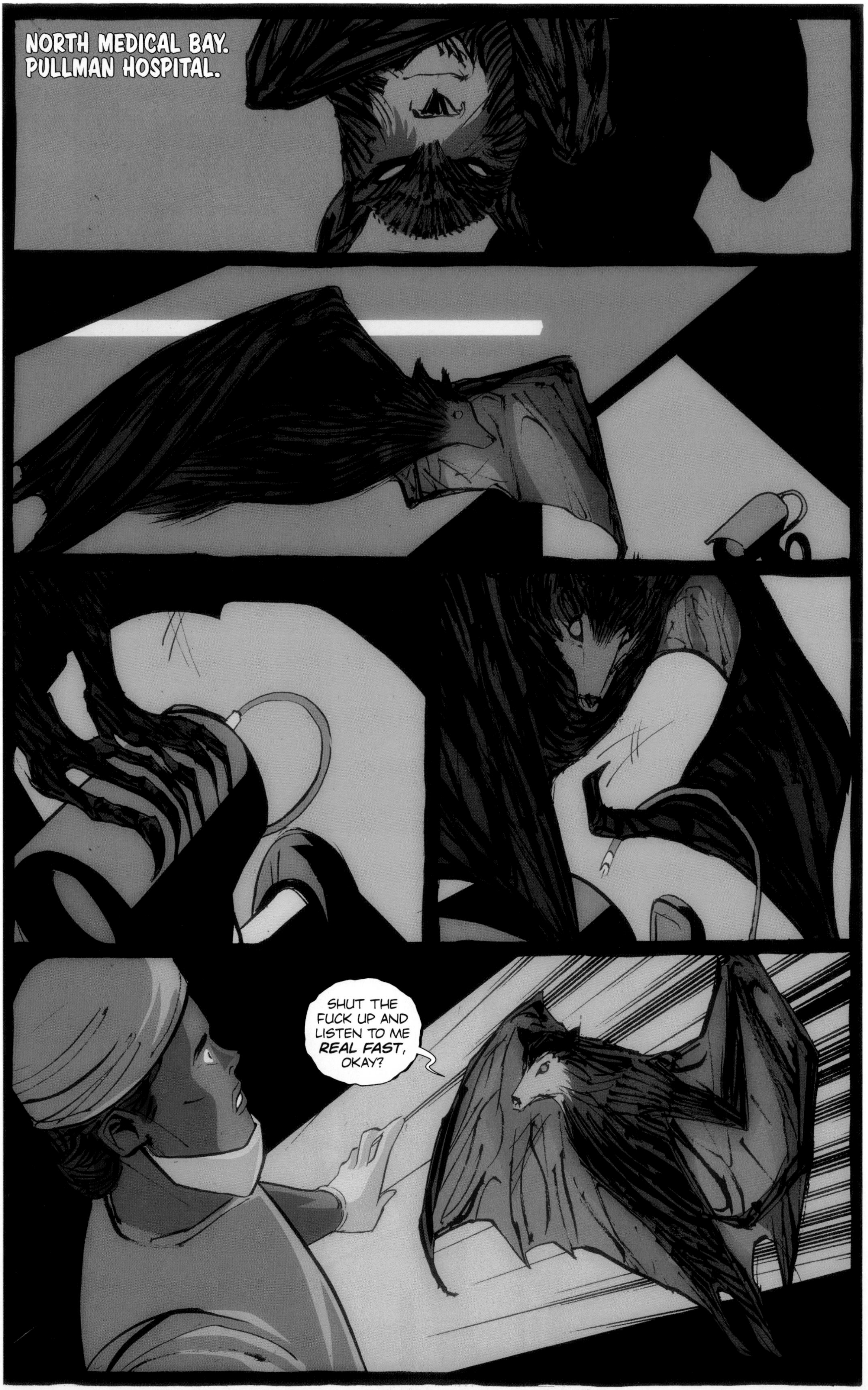
NORTH MEDICAL BAY.
PULLMAN HOSPITAL.
SHUT THE FUCK UP AND LISTEN TO ME REAL FAST, OKAY?

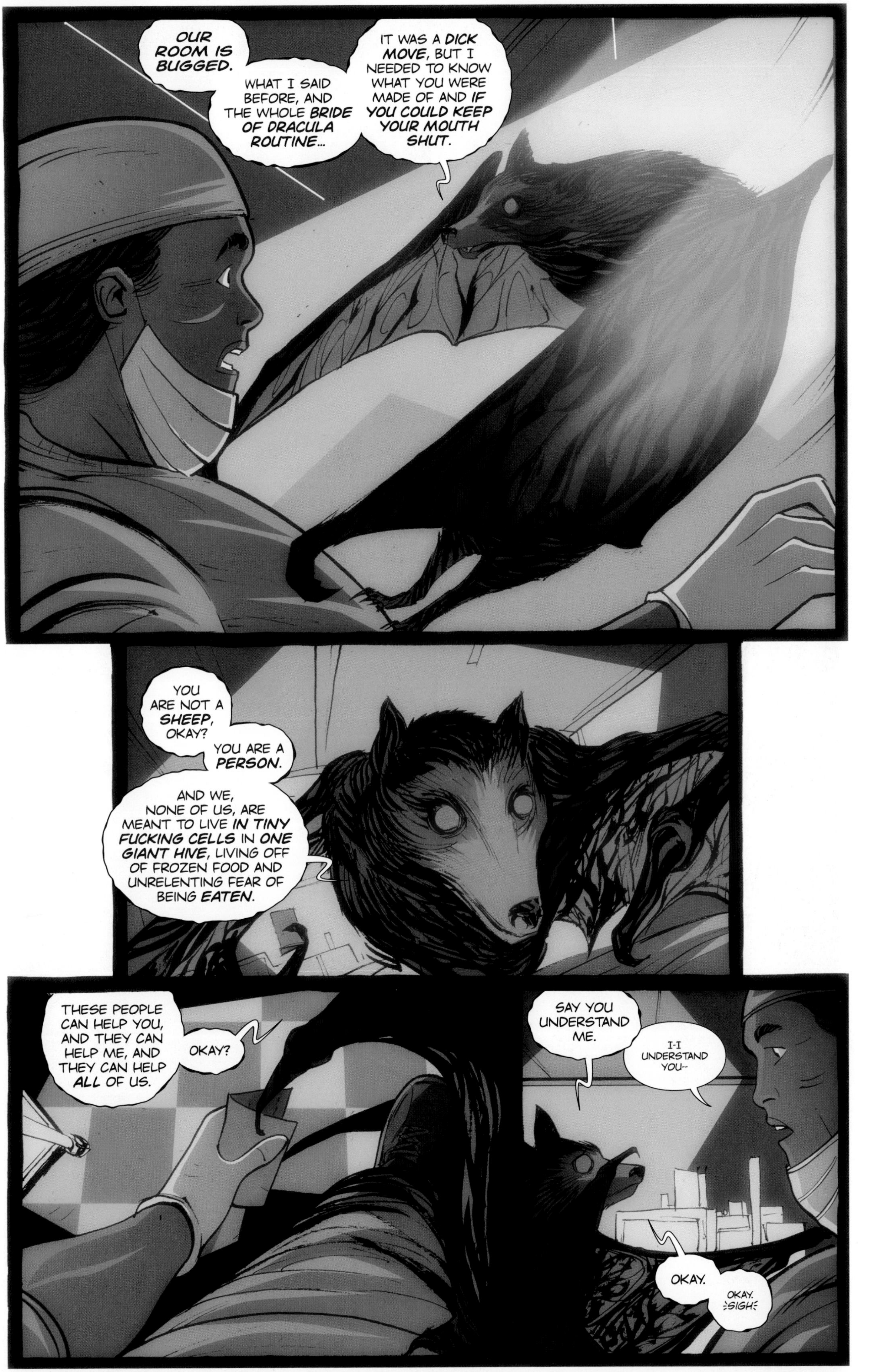

OUR ROOM IS BUGGED.
WHAT I SAID BEFORE, AND THE WHOLE BRIDE OF DRACULA ROUTINE...
IT WAS A DICK MOVE, BUT I NEEDED TO KNOW WHAT YOU WERE MADE OF AND IF YOU COULD KEEP YOUR MOUTH SHUT.
YOU ARE NOT A SHEEP, OKAY?
YOU ARE A PERSON.
AND WE, NONE OF US, ARE MEANT TO LIVE IN TINY FUCKING CELLS IN ONE GIANT HIVE, LIVING OFF OF FROZEN FOOD AND UNRELENTING FEAR OF BEING EATEN.
THESE PEOPLE CAN HELP YOU, AND THEY CAN HELP ME, AND THEY CAN HELP ALL OF US.
OKAY?
SAY YOU UNDERSTAND ME.
I-I UNDERSTAND YOU--
OKAY.
OKAY. SIGH

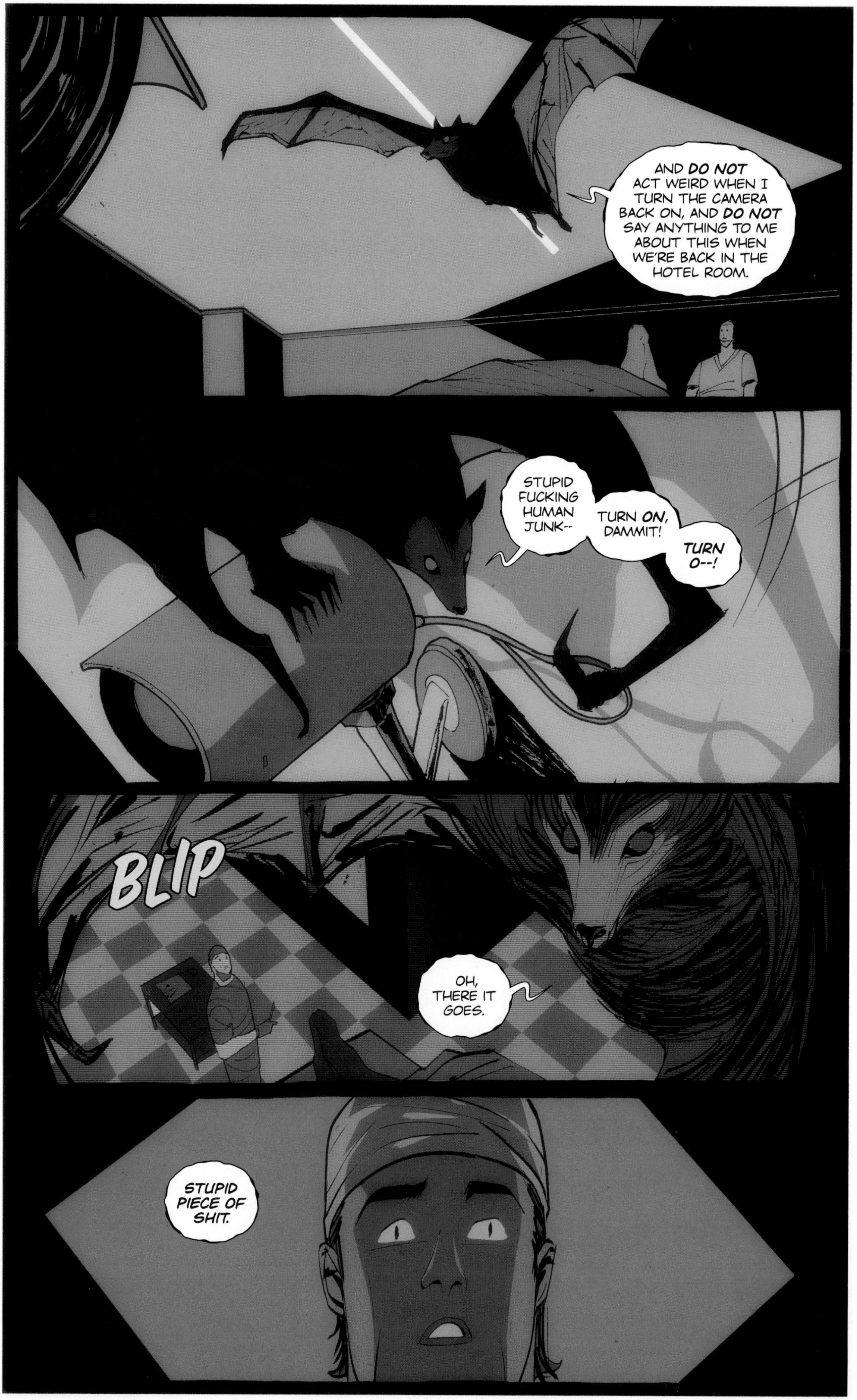
AND **DO NOT** ACT WEIRD WHEN I TURN THE CAMERA BACK ON, AND **DO NOT** SAY ANYTHING TO ME ABOUT THIS WHEN WE'RE BACK IN THE HOTEL ROOM.
STUPID FUCKING HUMAN JUNK--
TURN *ON*, DAMMIT!
TURN O--!
BLIP
OH, THERE IT GOES.
STUPID PIECE OF SHIT.

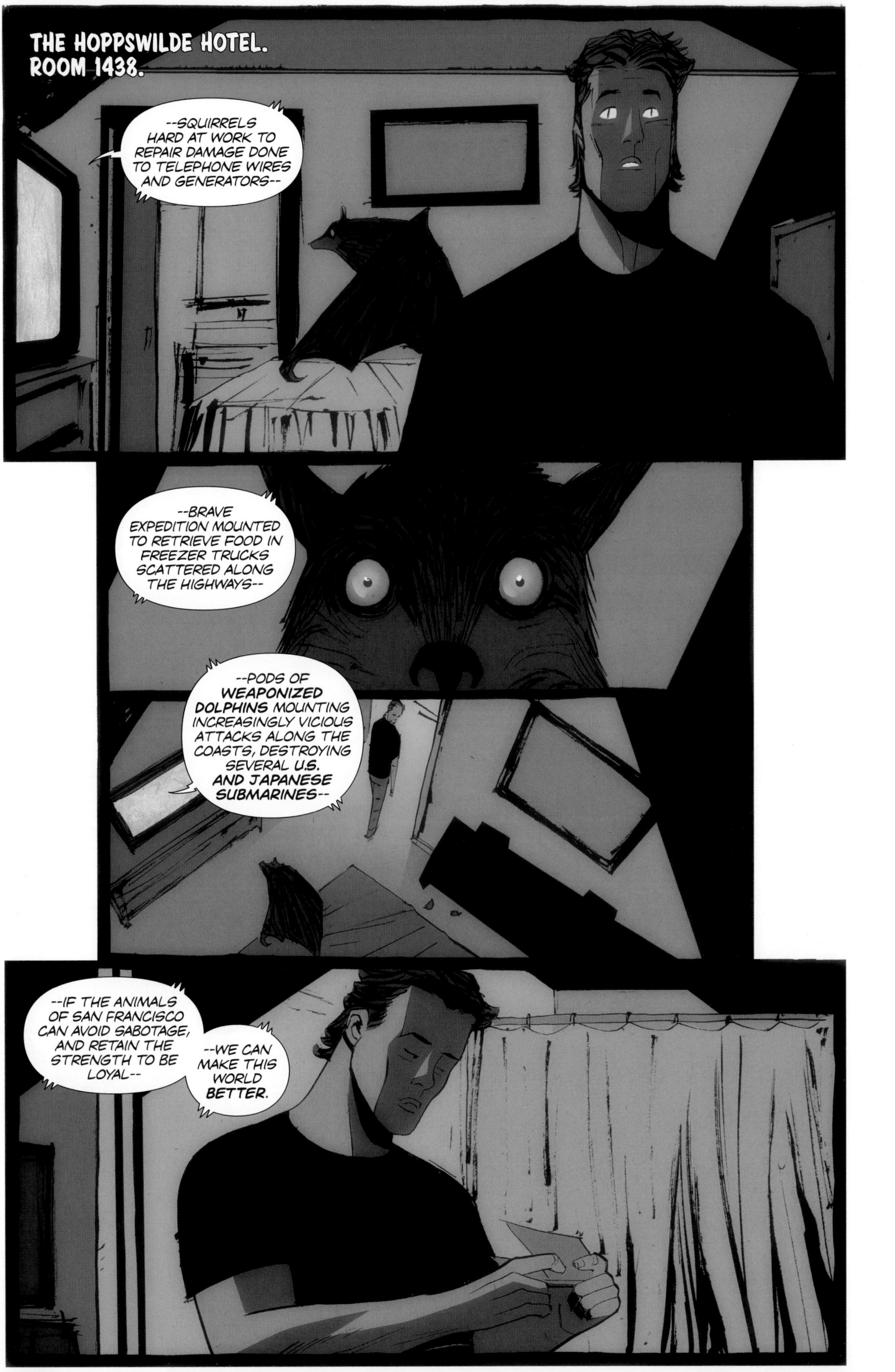

THE HOPPSWILDE HOTEL. ROOM 1438.
--SQUIRRELS HARD AT WORK TO REPAIR DAMAGE DONE TO TELEPHONE WIRES AND GENERATORS--
--BRAVE EXPEDITION MOUNTED TO RETRIEVE FOOD IN FREEZER TRUCKS SCATTERED ALONG THE HIGHWAYS--
--PODS OF **WEAPONIZED DOLPHINS** MOUNTING INCREASINGLY VICIOUS ATTACKS ALONG THE COASTS, DESTROYING SEVERAL **U.S.** **AND JAPANESE SUBMARINES**--
--IF THE ANIMALS OF SAN FRANCISCO CAN AVOID SABOTAGE, AND RETAIN THE STRENGTH TO BE LOYAL--
--WE CAN MAKE THIS WORLD **BETTER**.

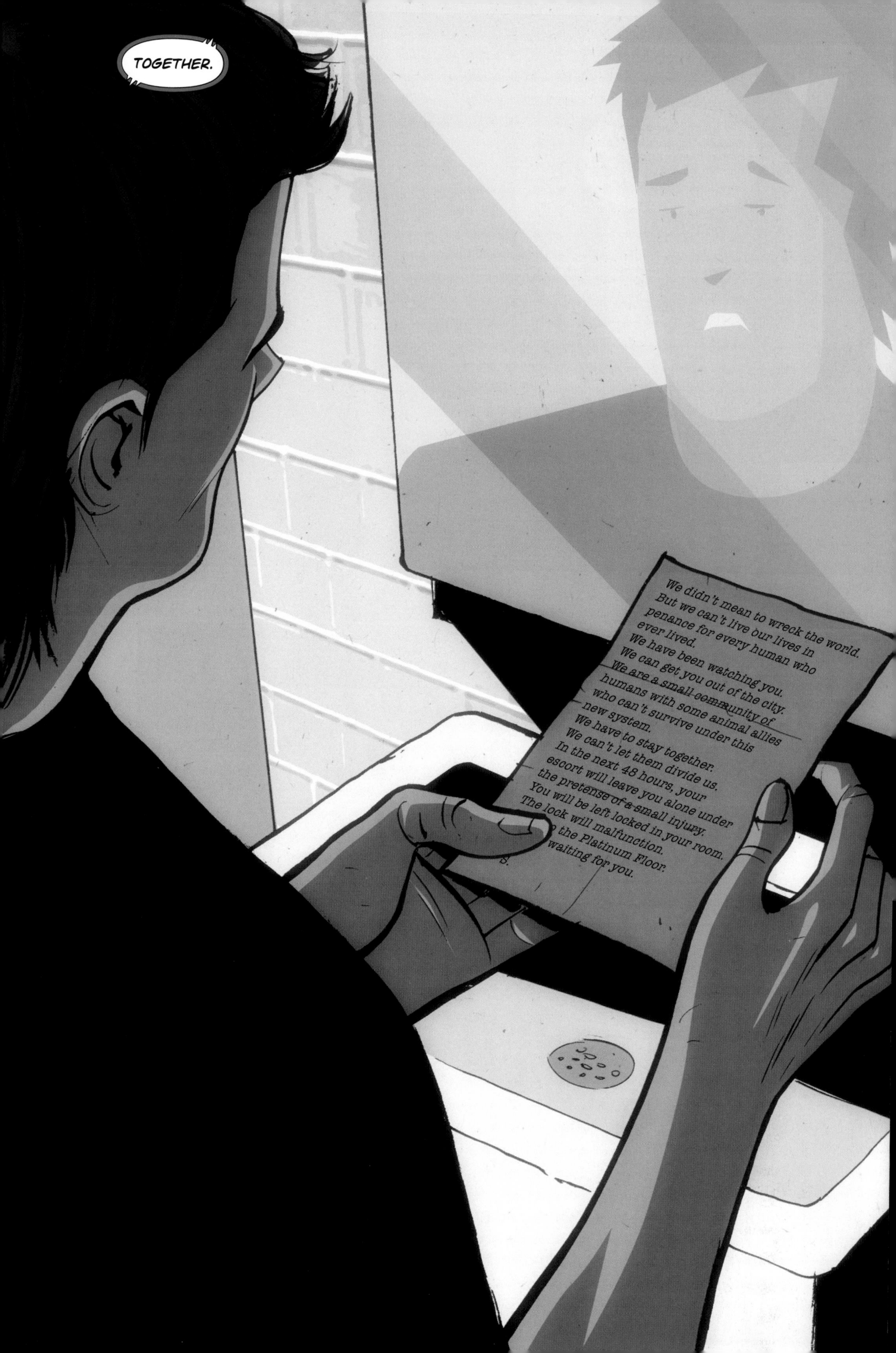
TOGETHER.
We didn't mean to wreck the world.
But we can't live our lives in
penance for every human who
ever lived.
We have been watching you.
We can get you out of the city.
We are a small community of
humans with some animal allies
who can't survive under this
new system.
We have to stay together.
We can't let them divide us.
In the next 48 hours, your
escort will leave you alone under
the pretense of a small injury.
You will be left locked in your room.
The lock will malfunction.
the Platinum Floor.
waiting for you.

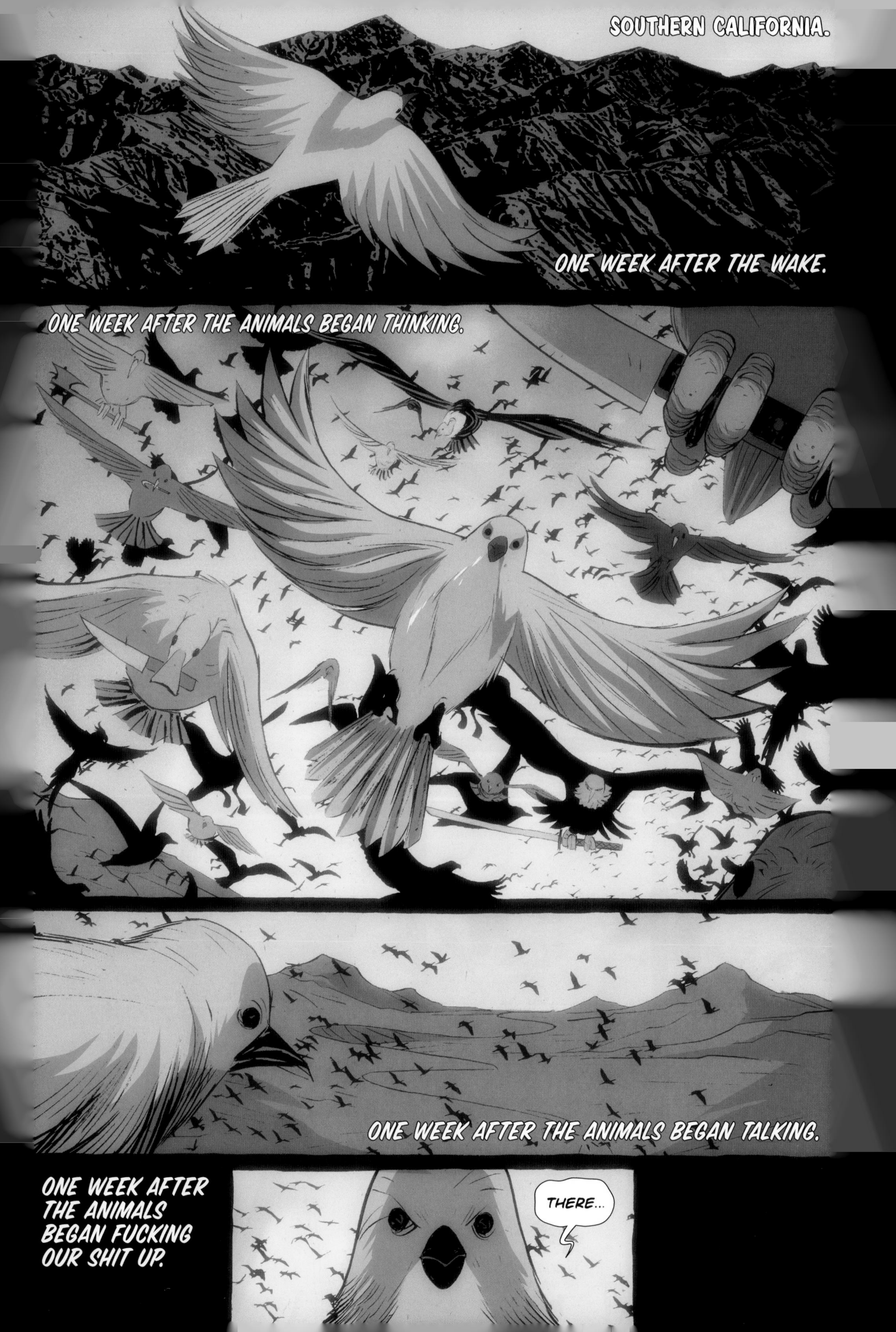

SOUTHERN CALIFORNIA.
ONE WEEK AFTER THE WAKE.
ONE WEEK AFTER THE ANIMALS BEGAN THINKING.
ONE WEEK AFTER THE ANIMALS BEGAN TALKING.
ONE WEEK AFTER THE ANIMALS BEGAN FUCKING OUR SHIT UP.
THERE...

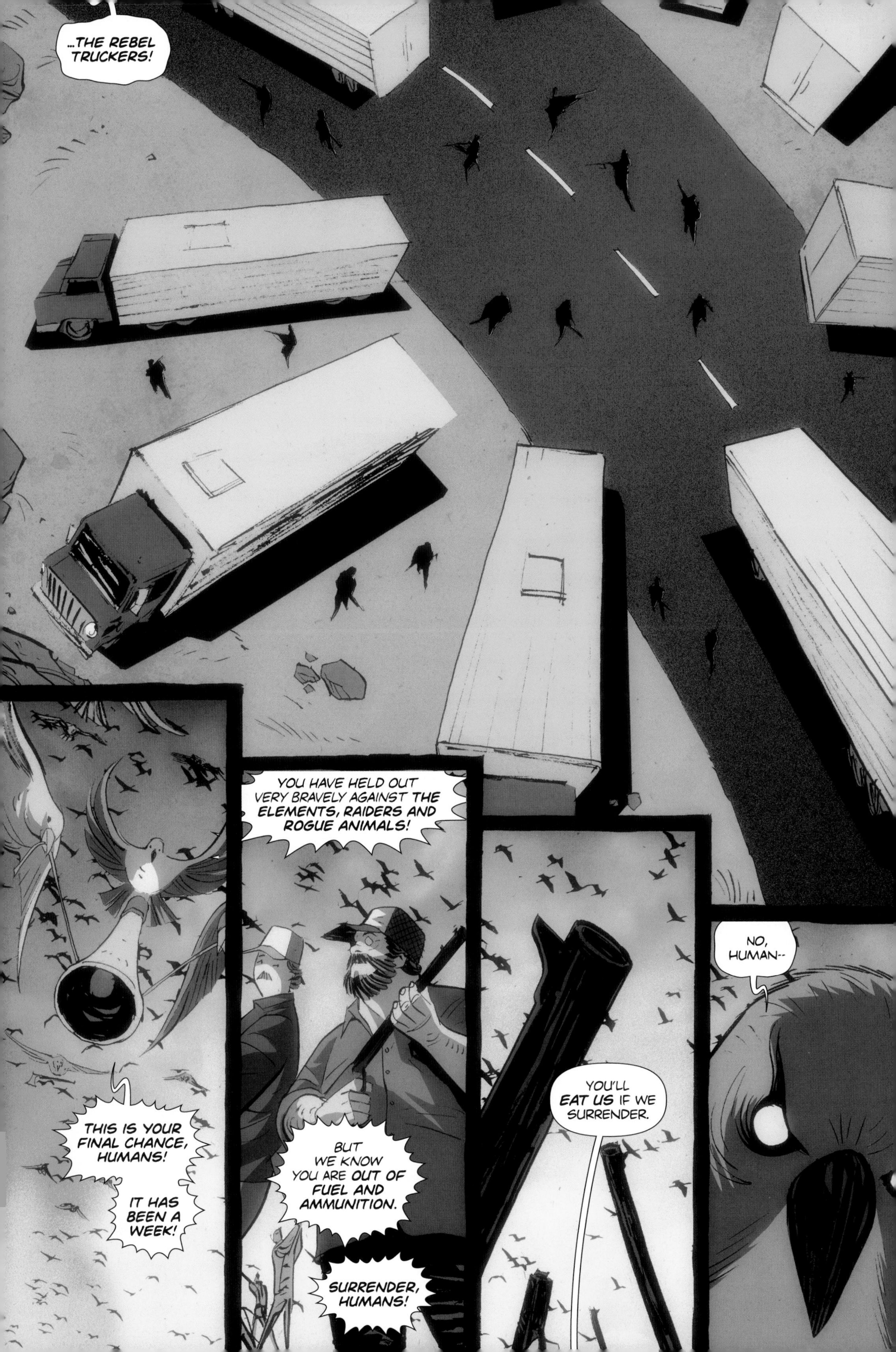
...THE REBEL TRUCKERS!
YOU HAVE HELD OUT VERY BRAVELY AGAINST THE ELEMENTS, RAIDERS AND ROGUE ANIMALS!
THIS IS YOUR FINAL CHANCE, HUMANS!
IT HAS BEEN A WEEK!
BUT WE KNOW YOU ARE OUT OF FUEL AND AMMUNITION.
SURRENDER, HUMANS!
YOU'LL EAT US IF WE SURRENDER.
NO, HUMAN--

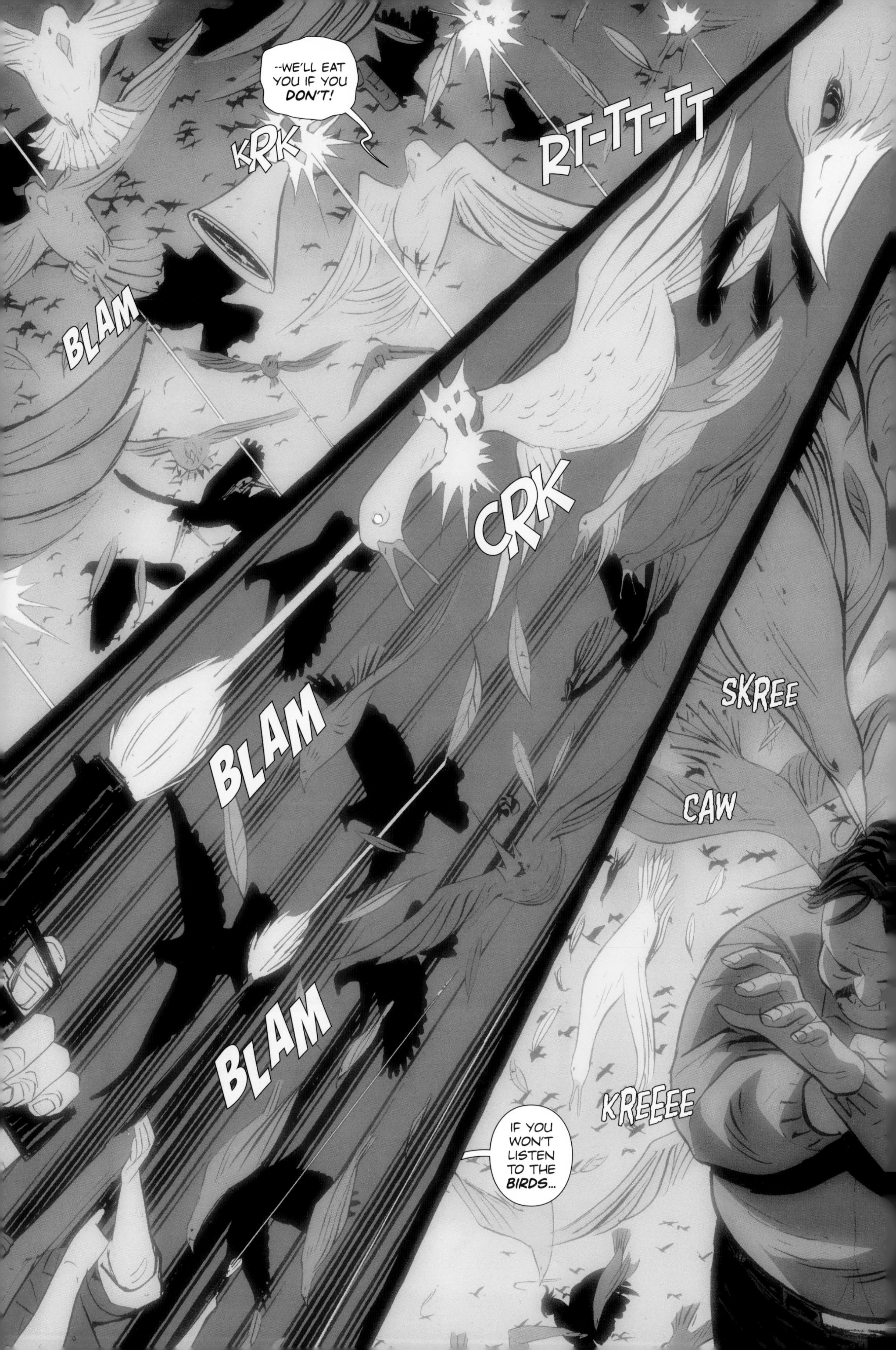

--WE'LL EAT YOU IF YOU DON'T!
KRK
RT-TT-TT
BLAM
CRK
BLAM
BLAM
SKREE
CAW
KREEEE
IF YOU WON'T LISTEN TO THE BIRDS...

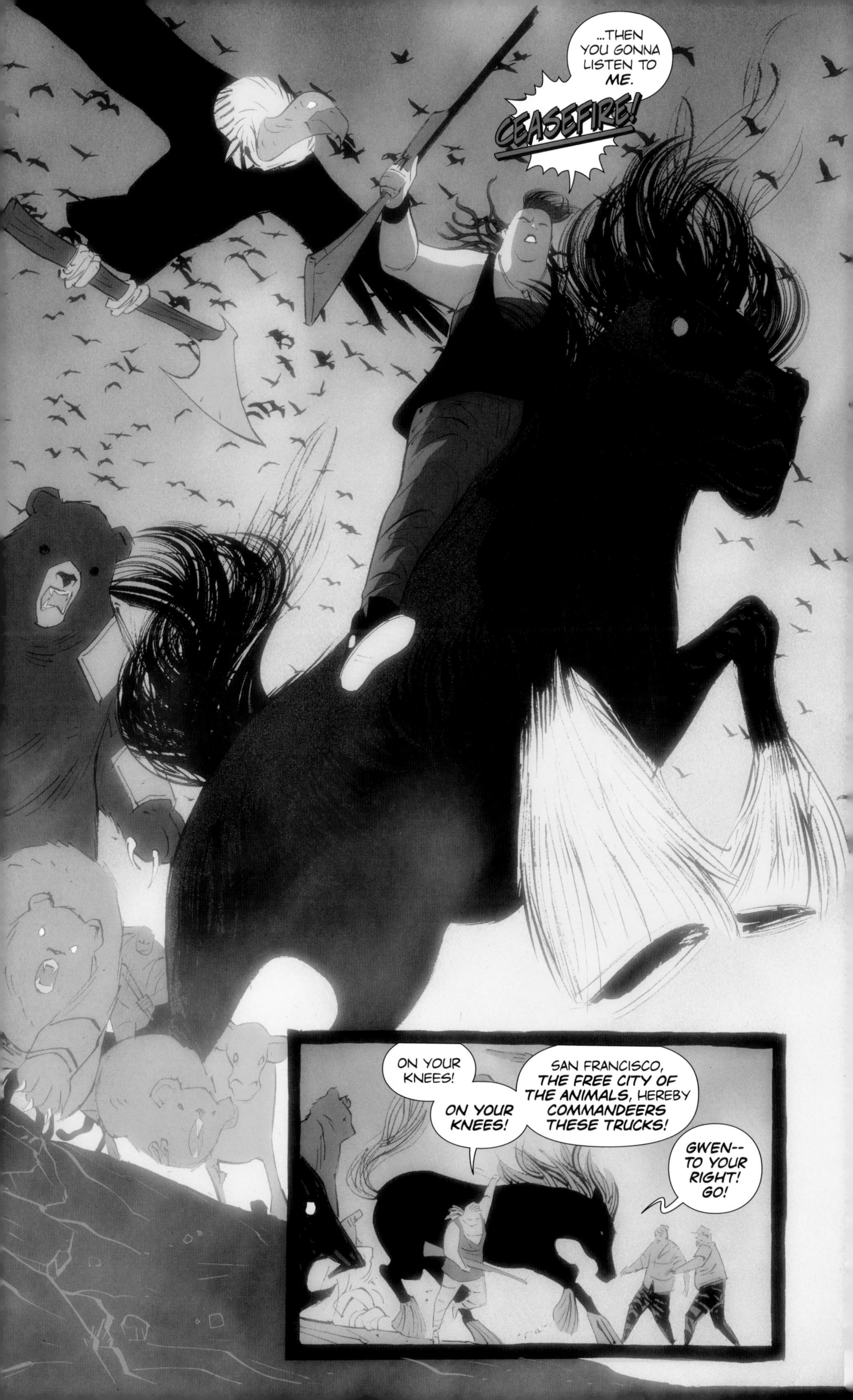
...THEN YOU GONNA LISTEN TO ME.
CEASEFIRE!
ON YOUR KNEES!
ON YOUR KNEES!
SAN FRANCISCO, THE FREE CITY OF THE ANIMALS, HEREBY COMMANDEERS THESE TRUCKS!
GWEN-- TO YOUR RIGHT! GO!

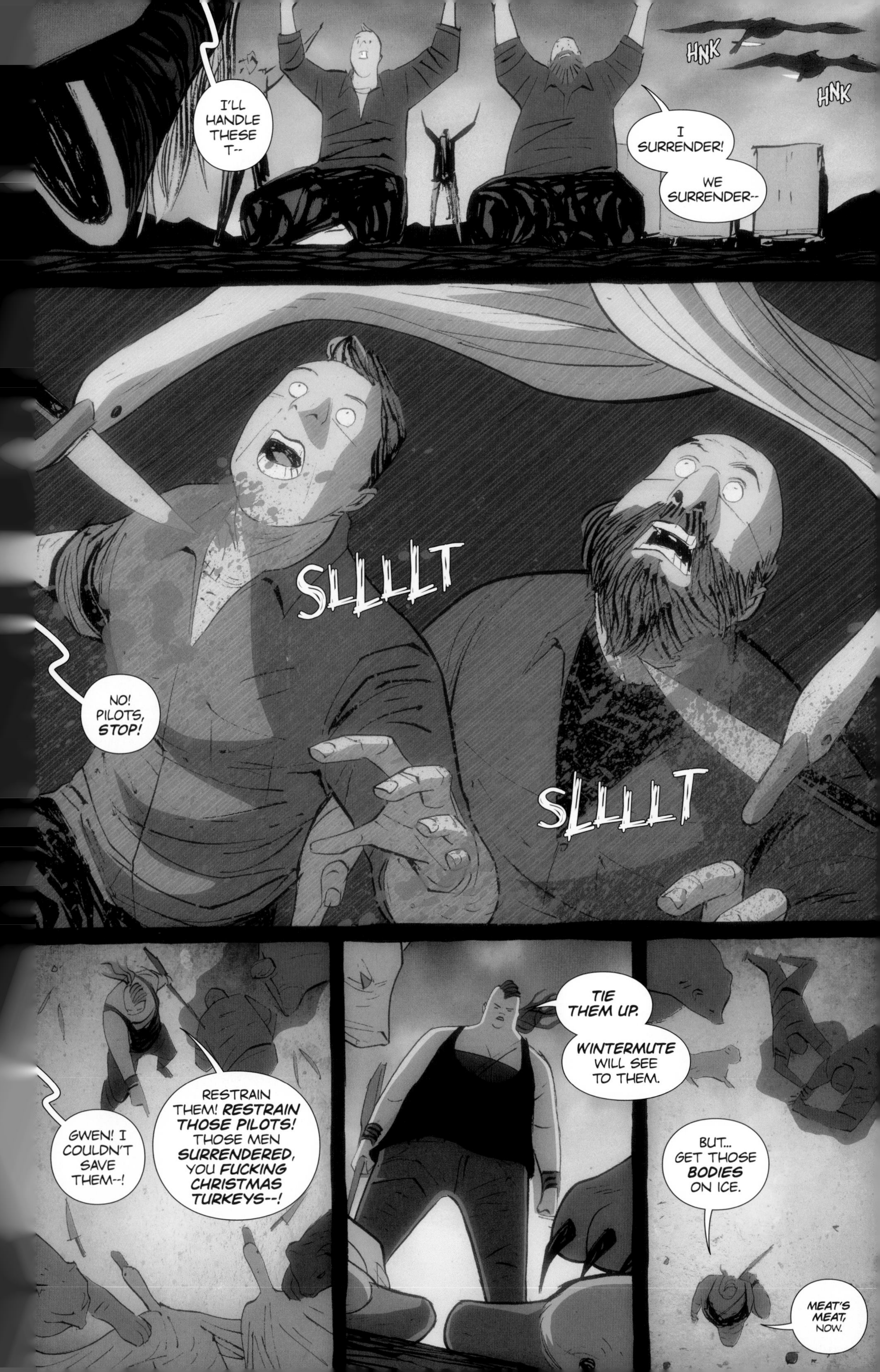
I'LL HANDLE THESE T--
HNK
HNK
I SURRENDER!
WE SURRENDER--
SLLLLT
SLLLLT
NO! PILOTS, STOP!
GWEN! I COULDN'T SAVE THEM--!
RESTRAIN THEM! RESTRAIN THOSE PILOTS! THOSE MEN SURRENDERED, YOU FUCKING CHRISTMAS TURKEYS--!
TIE THEM UP.
WINTERMUTE WILL SEE TO THEM.
BUT... GET THOSE BODIES ON ICE.
MEAT'S MEAT, NOW.

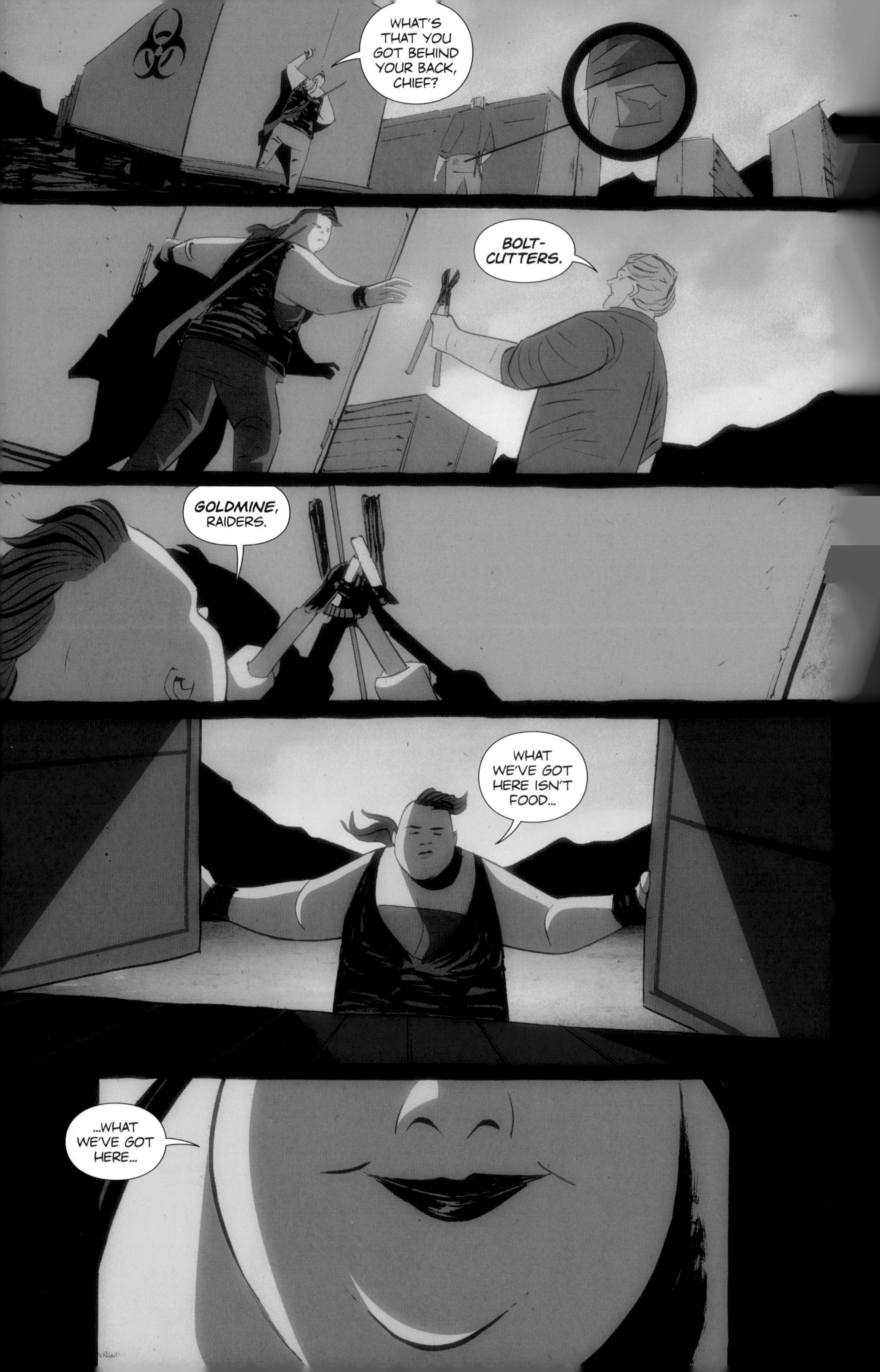
WHAT'S THAT YOU GOT BEHIND YOUR BACK, CHIEF?
BOLT-CUTTERS.
GOLDMINE, RAIDERS.
WHAT WE'VE GOT HERE ISN'T FOOD...
...WHAT WE'VE GOT HERE...

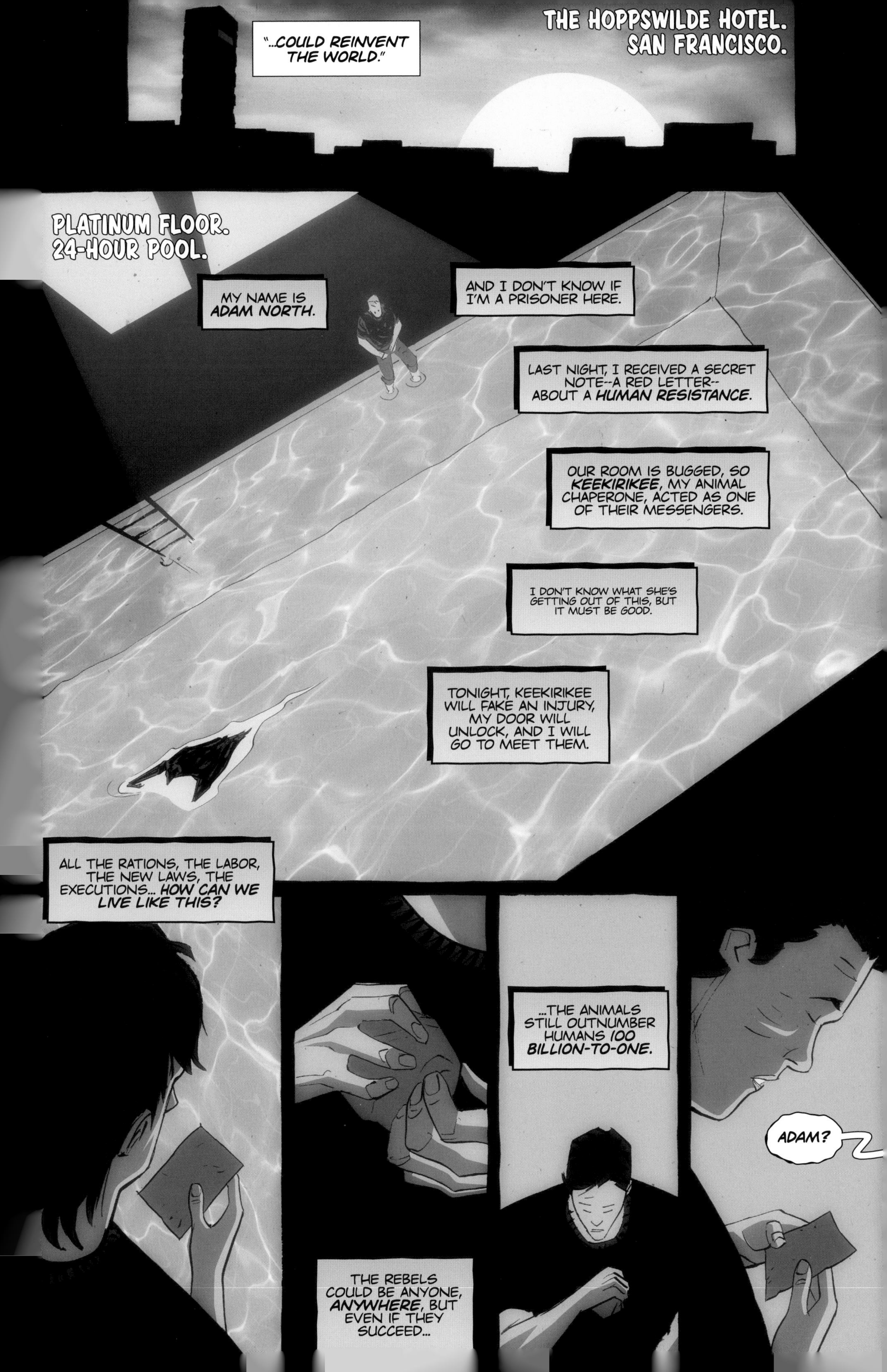
"...COULD REINVENT THE WORLD."
THE HOPPSWILDE HOTEL. SAN FRANCISCO.
PLATINUM FLOOR. 24-HOUR POOL.
MY NAME IS ADAM NORTH.
AND I DON'T KNOW IF I'M A PRISONER HERE.
LAST NIGHT, I RECEIVED A SECRET NOTE--A RED LETTER-- ABOUT A HUMAN RESISTANCE.
OUR ROOM IS BUGGED, SO KEEKIRIKEE, MY ANIMAL CHAPERONE, ACTED AS ONE OF THEIR MESSENGERS.
I DON'T KNOW WHAT SHE'S GETTING OUT OF THIS, BUT IT MUST BE GOOD.
TONIGHT, KEEKIRIKEE WILL FAKE AN INJURY, MY DOOR WILL UNLOCK, AND I WILL GO TO MEET THEM.
ALL THE RATIONS, THE LABOR, THE NEW LAWS, THE EXECUTIONS... HOW CAN WE LIVE LIKE THIS?
THE REBELS COULD BE ANYONE, ANYWHERE, BUT EVEN IF THEY SUCCEED...
...THE ANIMALS STILL OUTNUMBER HUMANS 100 BILLION-TO-ONE.
ADAM?

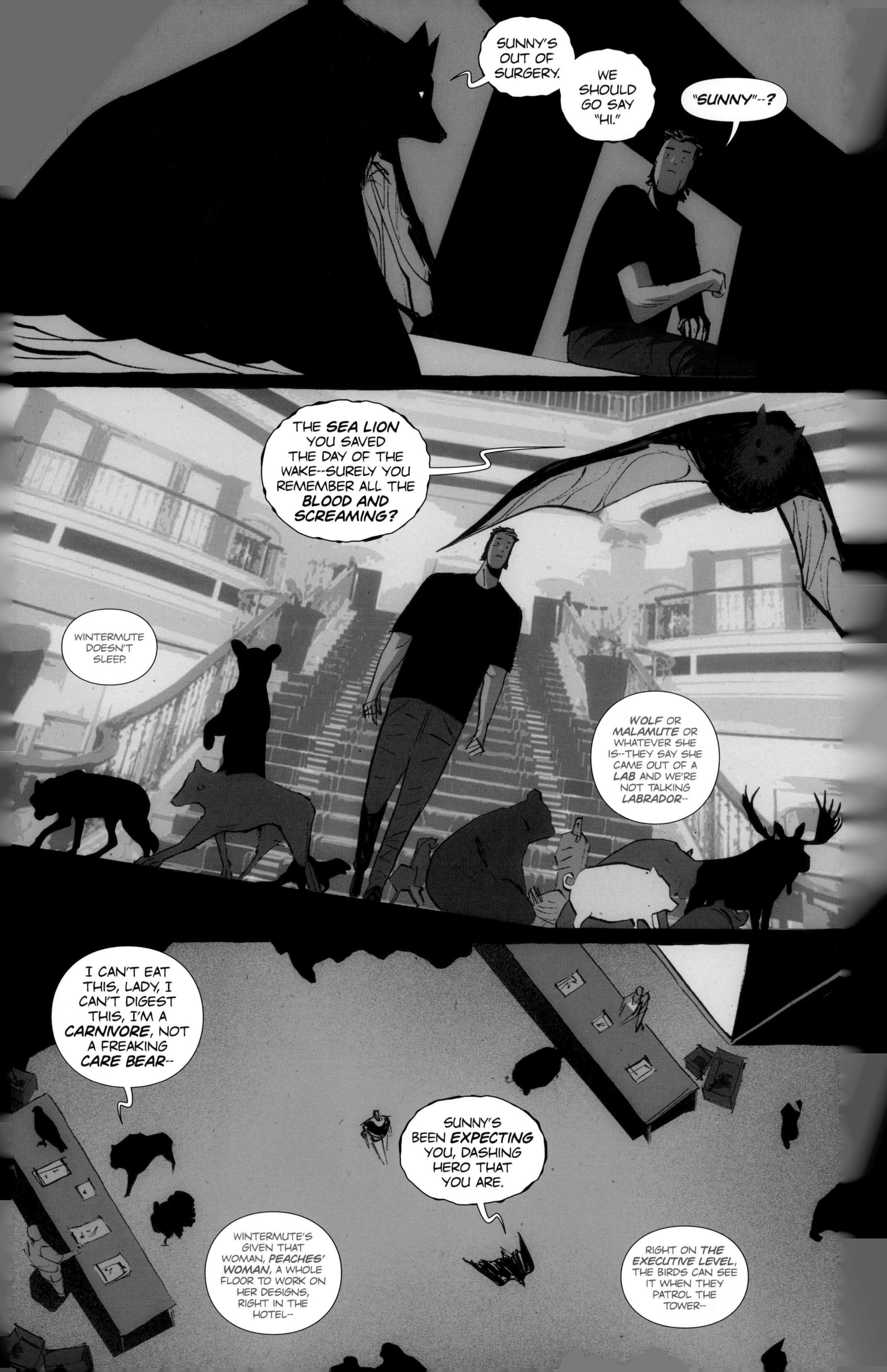
SUNNY'S OUT OF SURGERY.
WE SHOULD GO SAY "HI."
"SUNNY"--?
THE SEA LION YOU SAVED THE DAY OF THE WAKE--SURELY YOU REMEMBER ALL THE BLOOD AND SCREAMING?
WINTERMUTE DOESN'T SLEEP.
WOLF OR MALAMUTE OR WHATEVER SHE IS--THEY SAY SHE CAME OUT OF A LAB AND WE'RE NOT TALKING LABRADOR--
I CAN'T EAT THIS, LADY, I CAN'T DIGEST THIS, I'M A CARNIVORE, NOT A FREAKING CARE BEAR--
SUNNY'S BEEN EXPECTING YOU, DASHING HERO THAT YOU ARE.
WINTERMUTE'S GIVEN THAT WOMAN, PEACHES' WOMAN, A WHOLE FLOOR TO WORK ON HER DESIGNS, RIGHT IN THE HOTEL--
RIGHT ON THE EXECUTIVE LEVEL, THE BIRDS CAN SEE IT WHEN THEY PATROL THE TOWER--

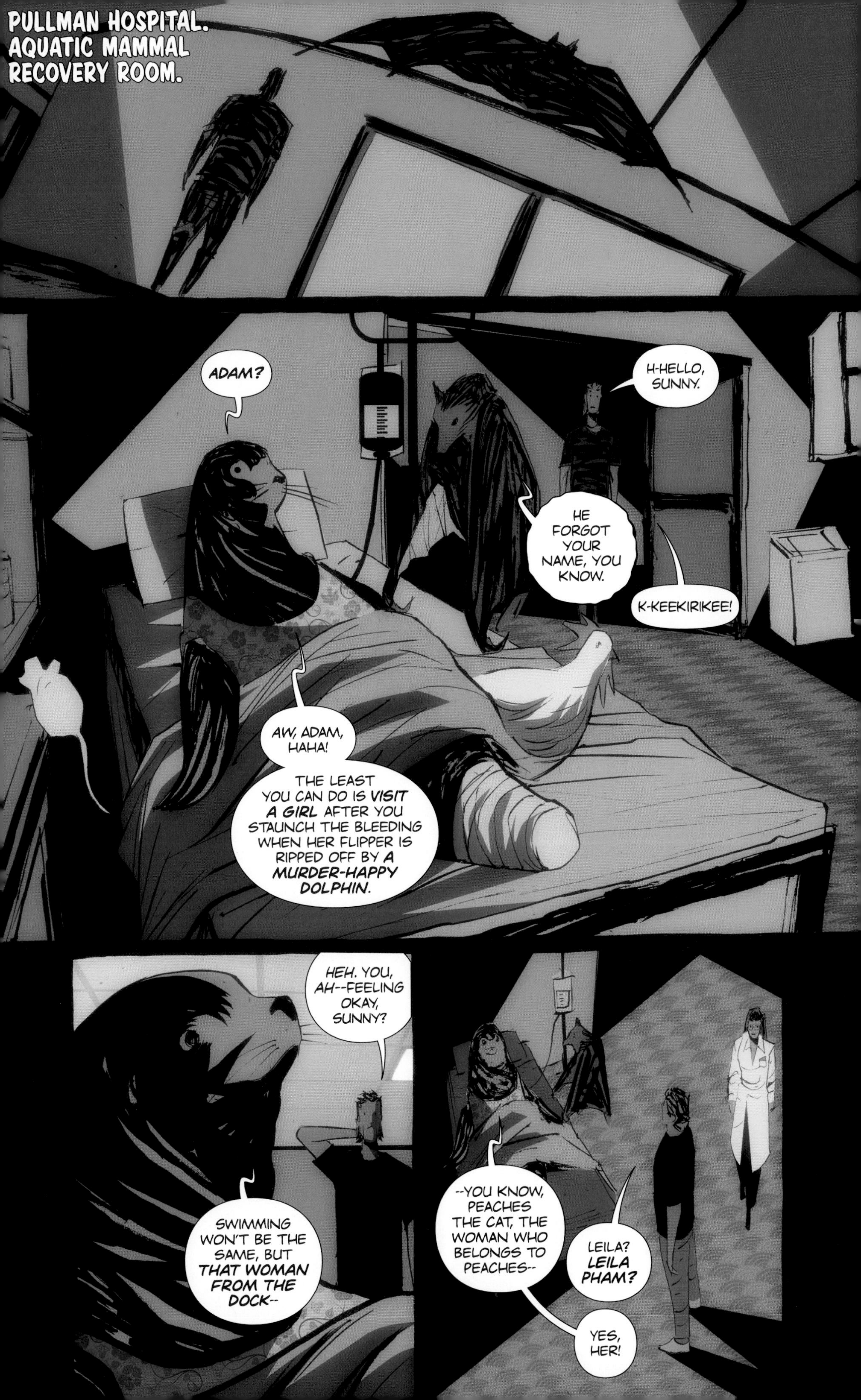
PULLMAN HOSPITAL. AQUATIC MAMMAL RECOVERY ROOM.
ADAM?
H-HELLO, SUNNY.
HE FORGOT YOUR NAME, YOU KNOW.
K-KEEKIRIKEE!
AW, ADAM, HAHA!
THE LEAST YOU CAN DO IS VISIT A GIRL AFTER YOU STAUNCH THE BLEEDING WHEN HER FLIPPER IS RIPPED OFF BY A MURDER-HAPPY DOLPHIN.
HEH. YOU, AH--FEELING OKAY, SUNNY?
SWIMMING WON'T BE THE SAME, BUT THAT WOMAN FROM THE DOCK--
--YOU KNOW, PEACHES THE CAT, THE WOMAN WHO BELONGS TO PEACHES--
LEILA? LEILA PHAM?
YES, HER!

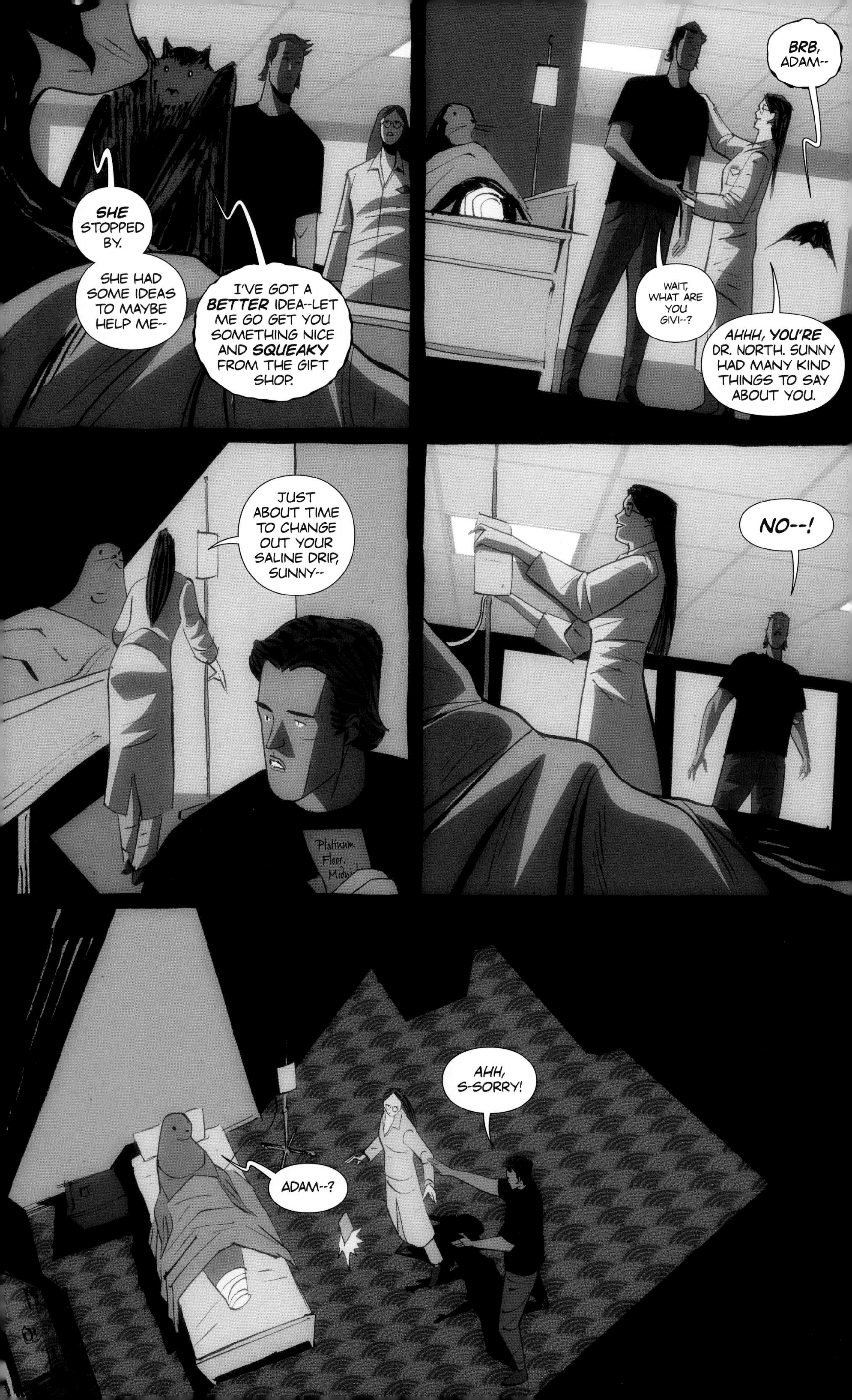

SHE STOPPED BY.
SHE HAD SOME IDEAS TO MAYBE HELP ME--
I'VE GOT A BETTER IDEA--LET ME GO GET YOU SOMETHING NICE AND SQUEAKY FROM THE GIFT SHOP.
BRB, ADAM--
WAIT, WHAT ARE YOU GIVI--?
AHHH, YOU'RE DR. NORTH. SUNNY HAD MANY KIND THINGS TO SAY ABOUT YOU.
JUST ABOUT TIME TO CHANGE OUT YOUR SALINE DRIP, SUNNY--
Platinum Floor. Midni
NO--!
AHH, S-SORRY!
ADAM--?

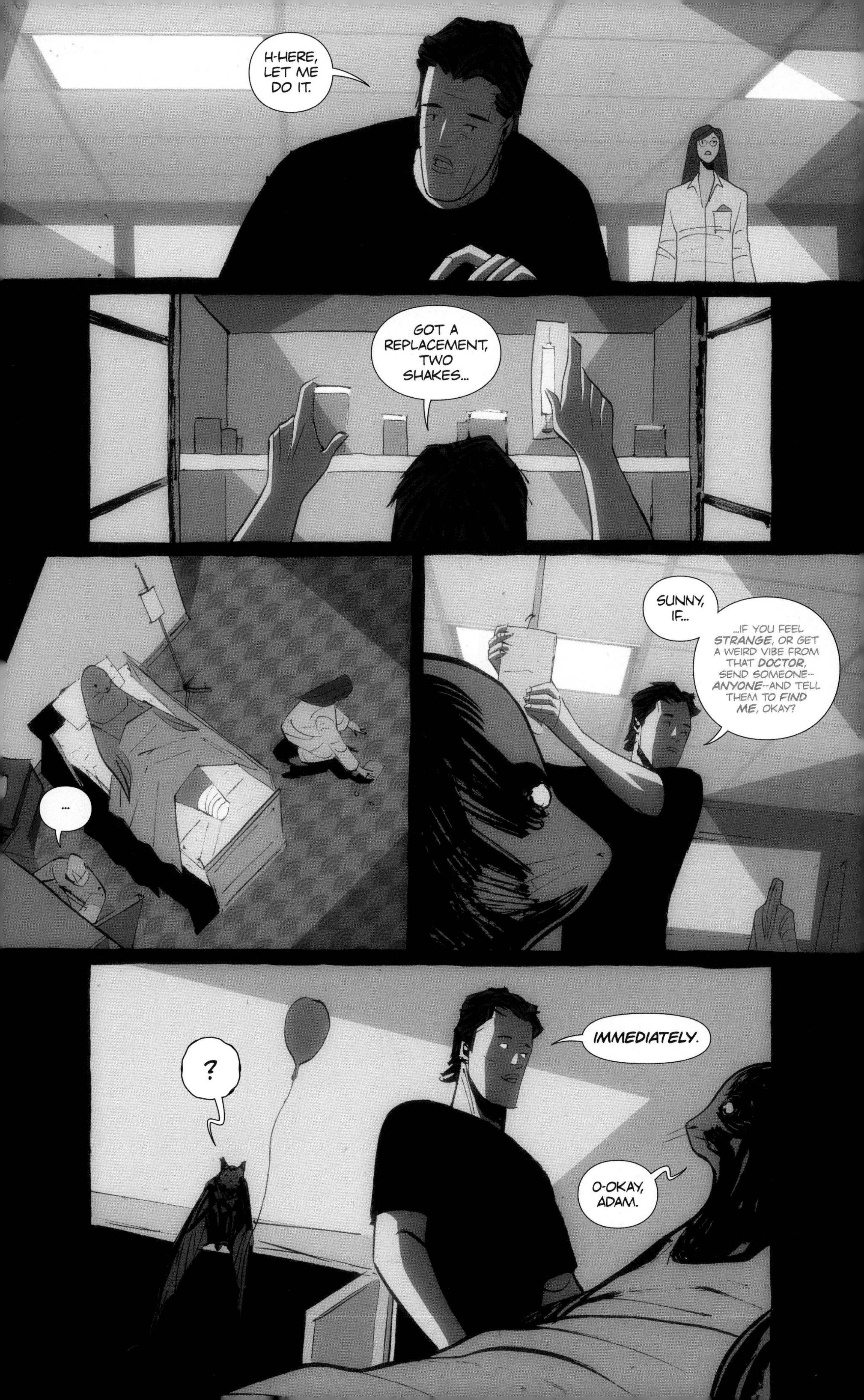
H-HERE, LET ME DO IT.
GOT A REPLACEMENT, TWO SHAKES...
...
SUNNY, IF...
...IF YOU FEEL STRANGE, OR GET A WEIRD VIBE FROM THAT DOCTOR, SEND SOMEONE--ANYONE--AND TELL THEM TO FIND ME, OKAY?
?
IMMEDIATELY.
O-OKAY, ADAM.

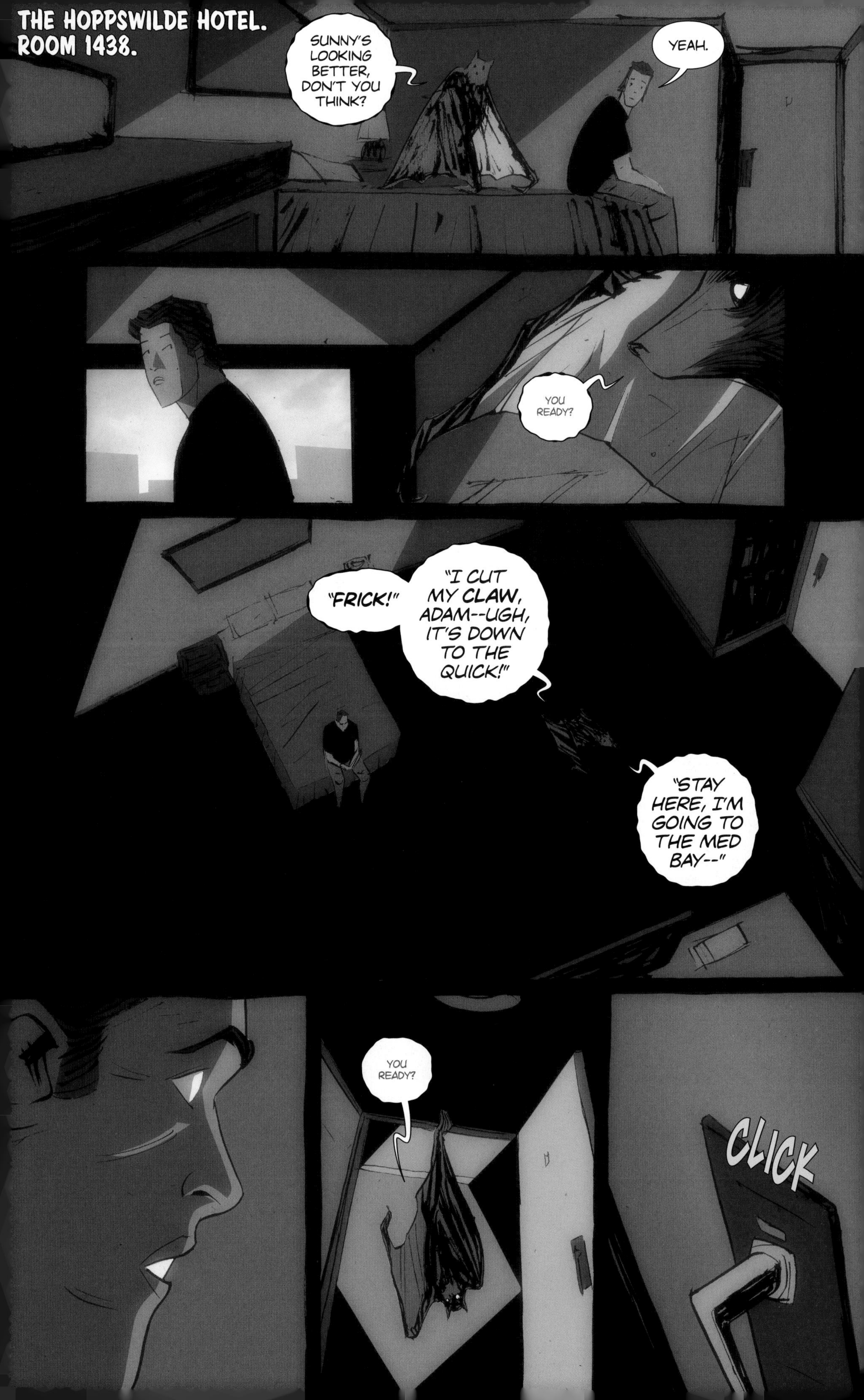
THE HOPPSWILDE HOTEL. ROOM 1438.
SUNNY'S LOOKING BETTER, DON'T YOU THINK?
YEAH.
YOU READY?
"FRICK!"
"I CUT MY CLAW, ADAM--UGH, IT'S DOWN TO THE QUICK!"
"STAY HERE, I'M GOING TO THE MED BAY--"
YOU READY?
CLICK

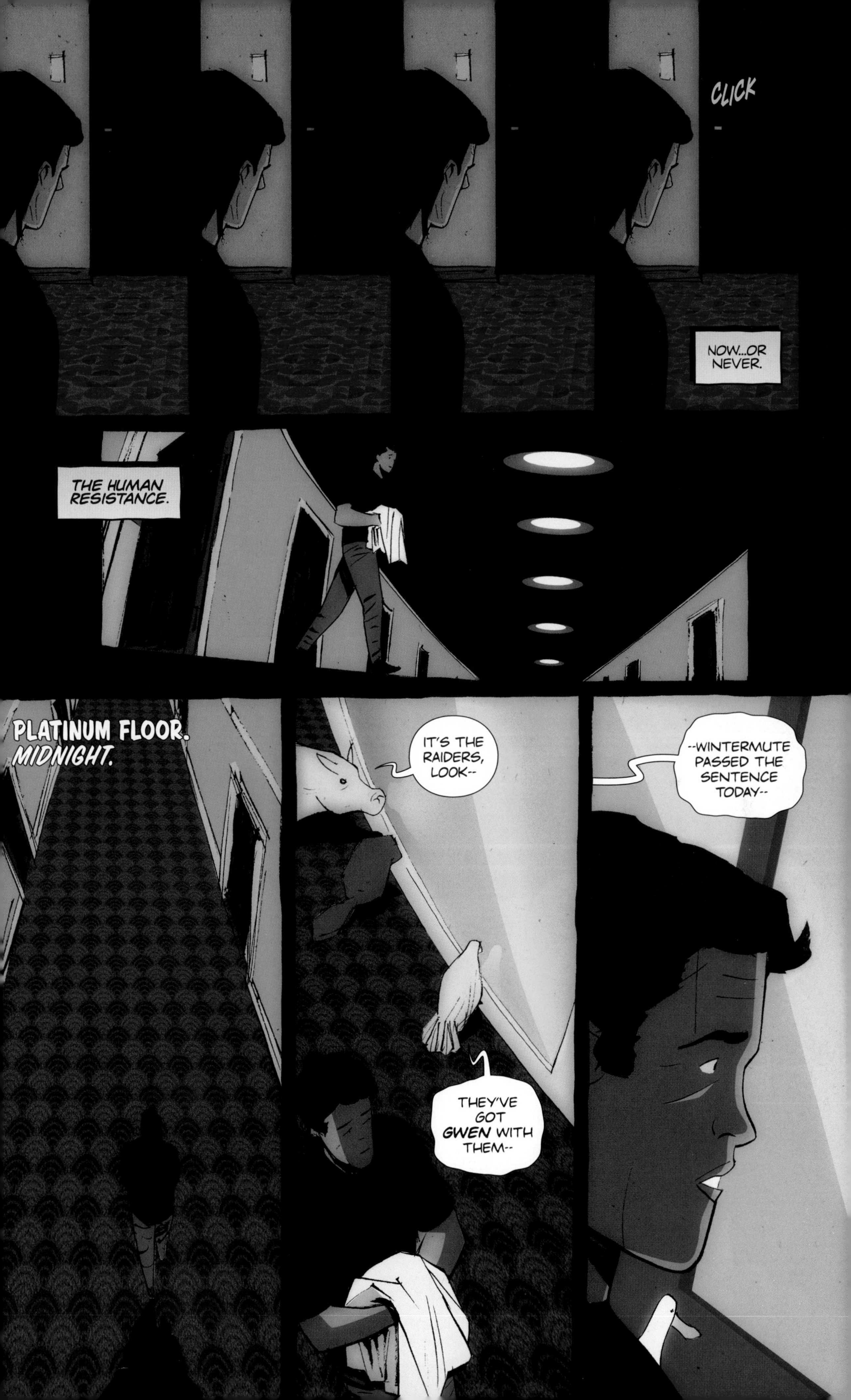
CLICK
NOW...OR NEVER.
THE HUMAN RESISTANCE.
PLATINUM FLOOR. MIDNIGHT.
IT'S THE RAIDERS, LOOK--
THEY'VE GOT GWEN WITH THEM--
--WINTERMUTE PASSED THE SENTENCE TODAY--

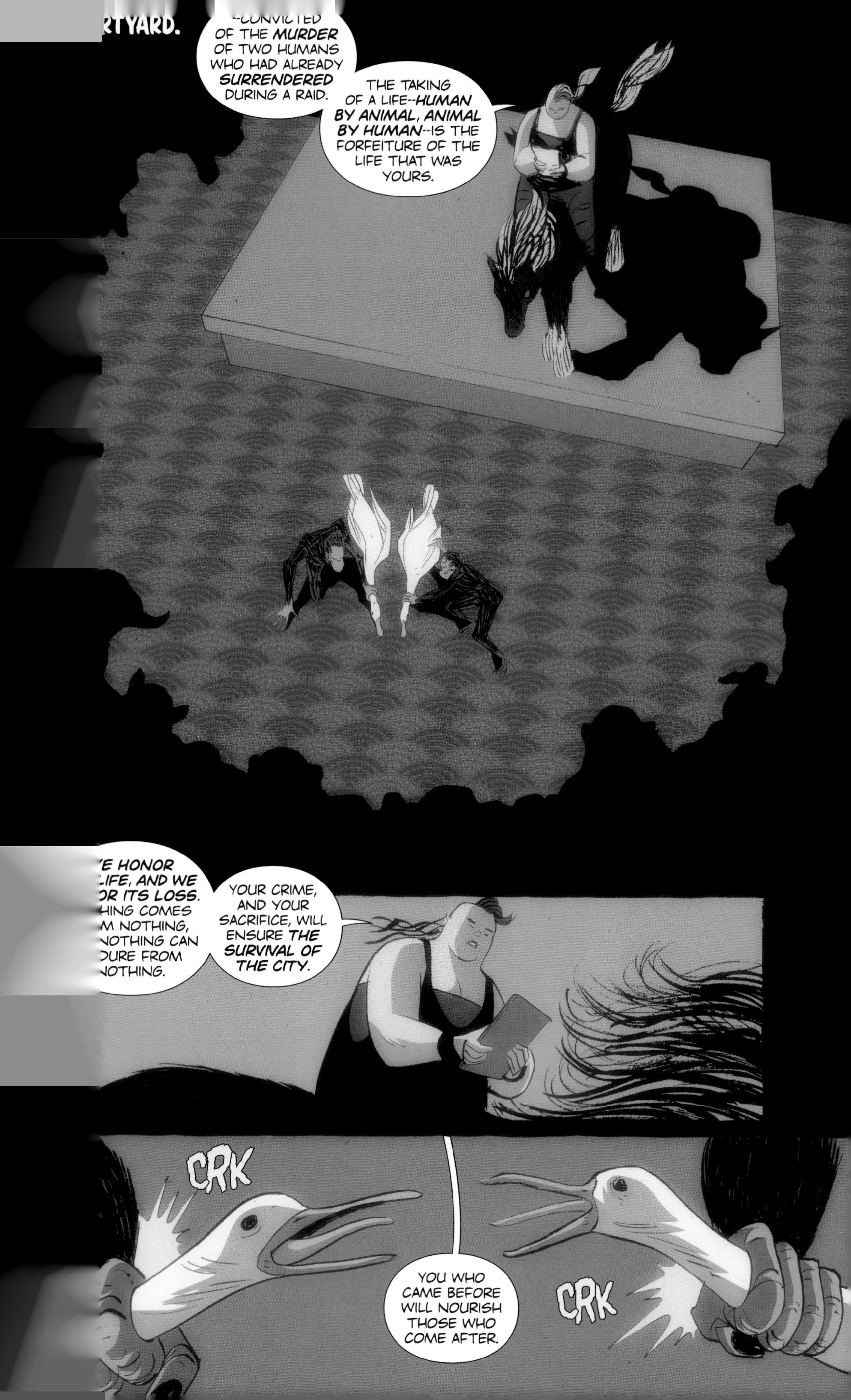
RTYARD.
--CONVICTED OF THE MURDER OF TWO HUMANS WHO HAD ALREADY SURRENDERED DURING A RAID.
THE TAKING OF A LIFE--HUMAN BY ANIMAL, ANIMAL BY HUMAN--IS THE FORFEITURE OF THE LIFE THAT WAS YOURS.
E HONOR LIFE, AND WE OR ITS LOSS. HING COMES M NOTHING, NOTHING CAN DURE FROM NOTHING.
YOUR CRIME, AND YOUR SACRIFICE, WILL ENSURE THE SURVIVAL OF THE CITY.
CRK
YOU WHO CAME BEFORE WILL NOURISH THOSE WHO COME AFTER.
CRK

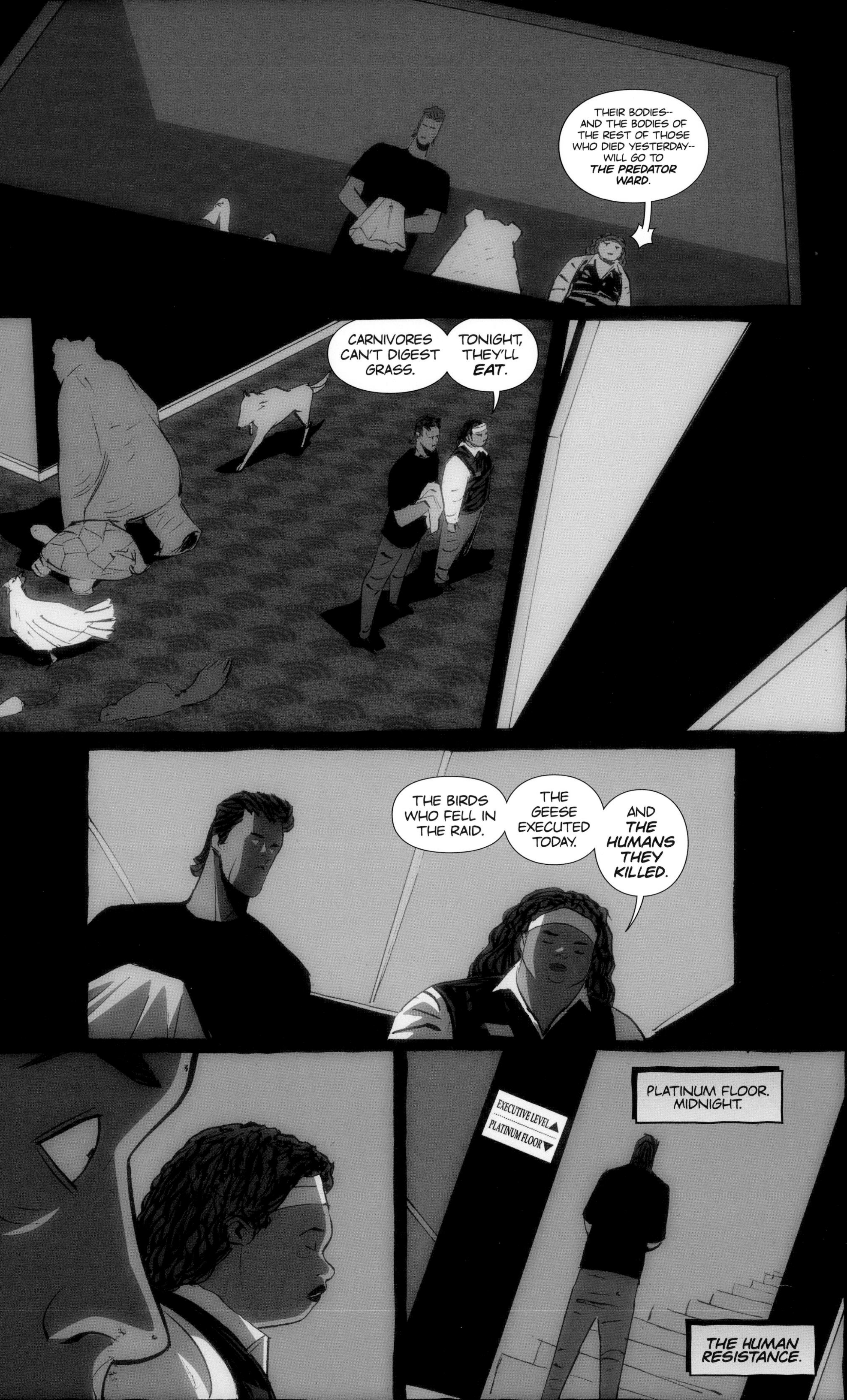
THEIR BODIES-- AND THE BODIES OF THE REST OF THOSE WHO DIED YESTERDAY-- WILL GO TO **THE PREDATOR WARD**.
CARNIVORES CAN'T DIGEST GRASS.
TONIGHT, THEY'LL **EAT**.
THE BIRDS WHO FELL IN THE RAID.
THE GEESE EXECUTED TODAY.
AND **THE HUMANS THEY KILLED**.
EXECUTIVE LEVEL
PLATINUM FLOOR
PLATINUM FLOOR. MIDNIGHT.
THE HUMAN RESISTANCE.

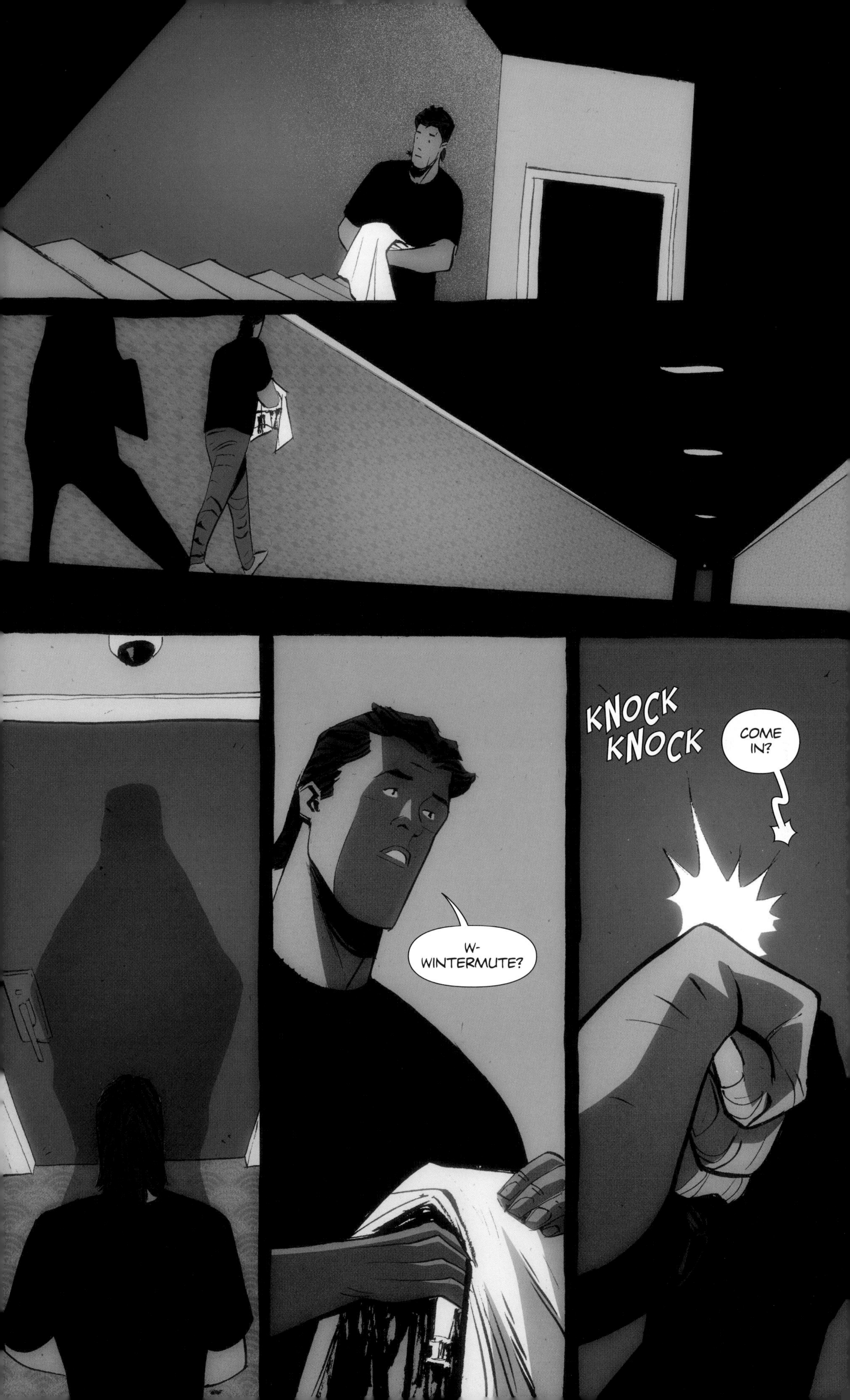
W-
WINTERMUTE?
KNOCK
KNOCK
COME
IN?

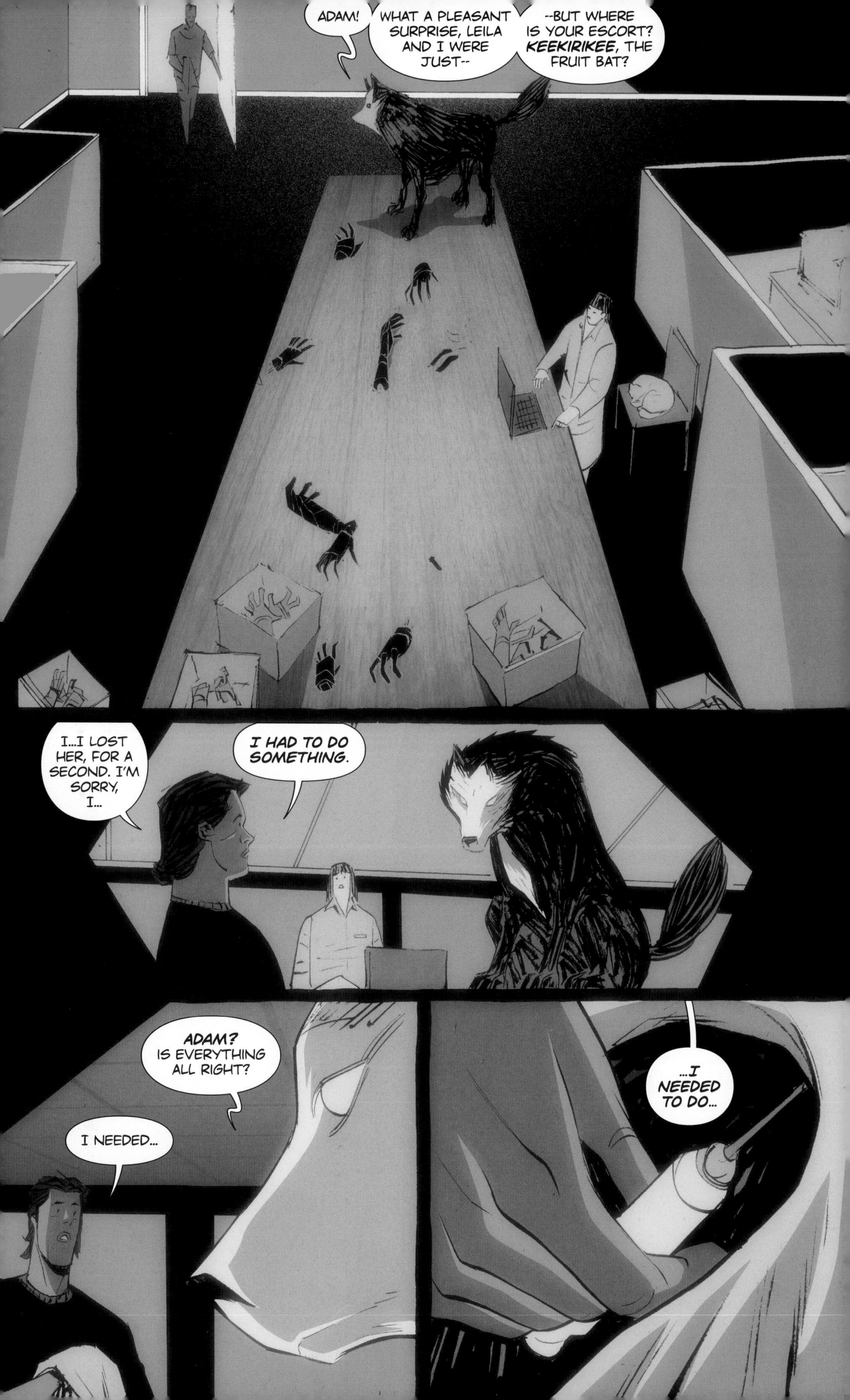
ADAM!
WHAT A PLEASANT SURPRISE, LEILA AND I WERE JUST--
--BUT WHERE IS YOUR ESCORT? KEEKIRIKEE, THE FRUIT BAT?
I...I LOST HER, FOR A SECOND. I'M SORRY, I...
I HAD TO DO SOMETHING.
ADAM? IS EVERYTHING ALL RIGHT?
I NEEDED...
...I NEEDED TO DO...

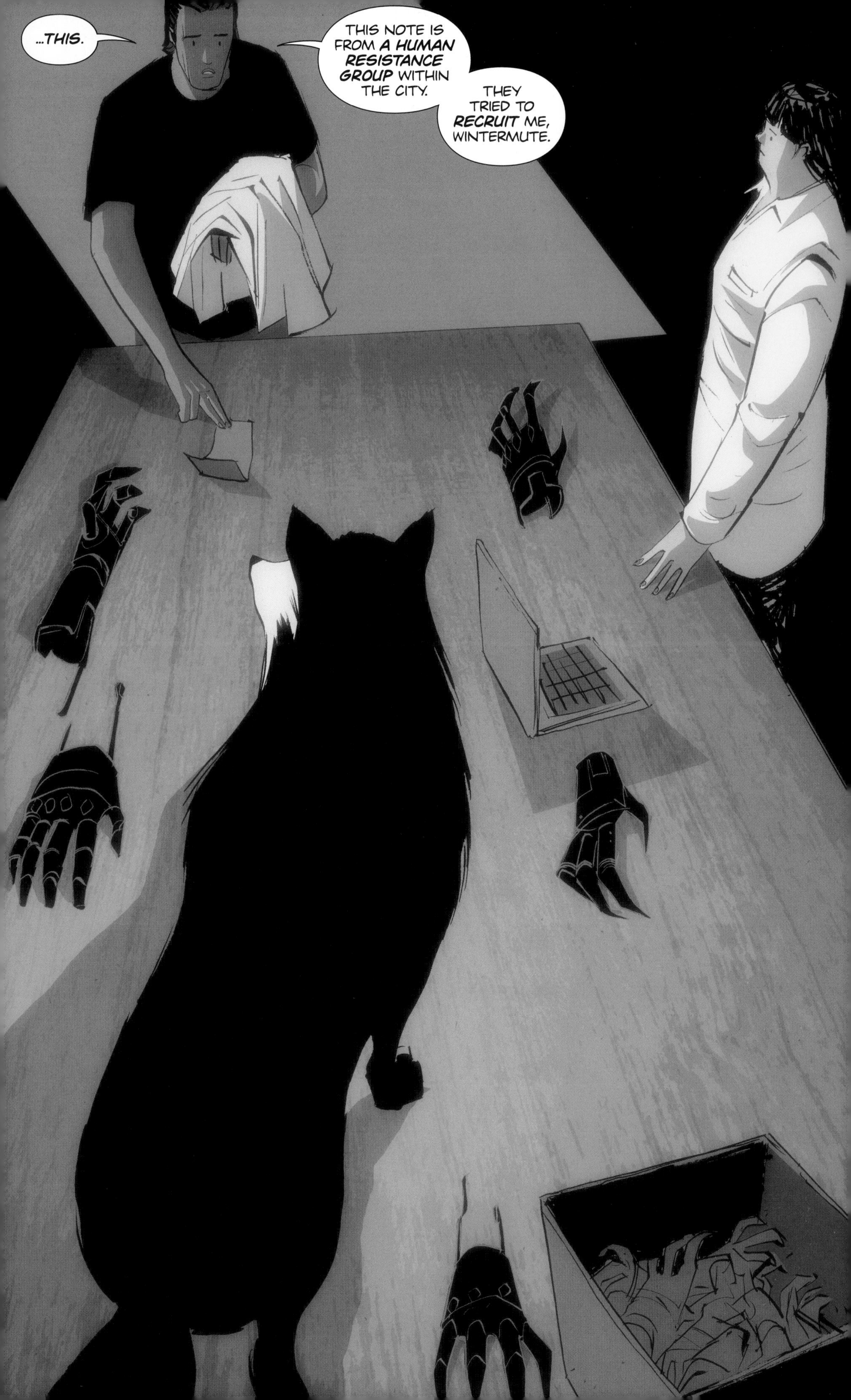
...THIS.
THIS NOTE IS FROM A HUMAN RESISTANCE GROUP WITHIN THE CITY.
THEY TRIED TO RECRUIT ME, WINTERMUTE.

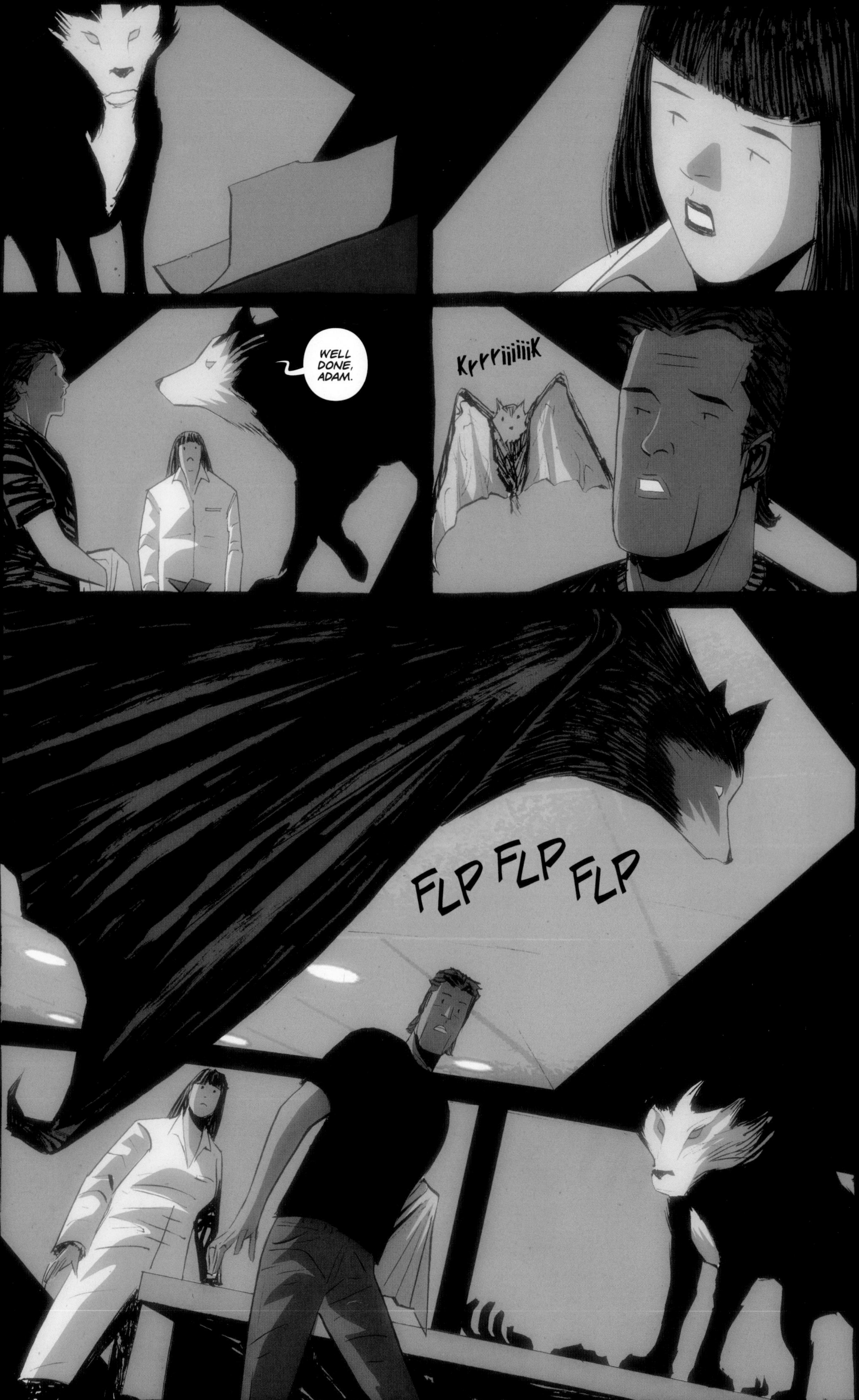
WELL DONE, ADAM.
KRRRIIIIIK
FLP FLP FLP

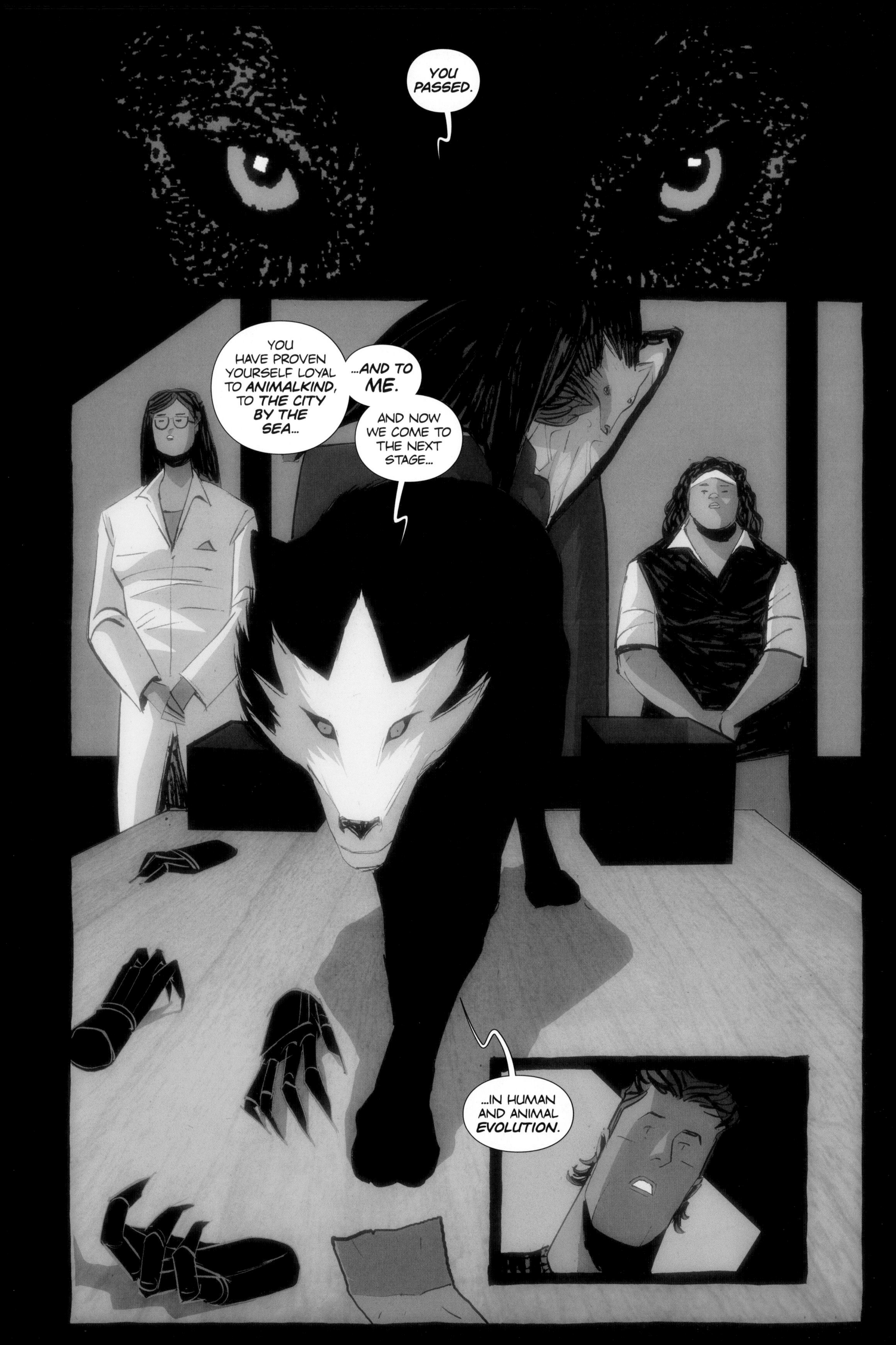
YOU PASSED.
YOU HAVE PROVEN YOURSELF LOYAL TO ANIMALKIND, TO THE CITY BY THE SEA...
...AND TO ME.
AND NOW WE COME TO THE NEXT STAGE...
...IN HUMAN AND ANIMAL EVOLUTION.

CHECK OUT THESE GREAT AFTERSHOCK
COLLECTIONS!

MARGUERITE BENNETT
writer
🐦 @EvilMarguerite

Marguerite Bennett is a comic book writer from Richmond, Virginia, who currently splits her time between Los Angeles and New York City. She received her MFA in Creative Writing from Sarah Lawrence College in 2013 and quickly went on to work for DC Comics, Marvel, BOOM! Studios, Dynamite and IDW on projects ranging from *Batman, Bombshells* and *A-Force* to *Angela: Asgard's Assassin, Red Sonja* and FOX TV's *Sleepy Hollow.*

JUAN DOE
artist
🐦 @juandoe

Juan Doe is a professional illustrator with over ten years experience in the comic book industry. He has produced over a hundred covers and his sequential highlights include the *Fantastic Four in Puerto Rico* trilogy, *The Legion of Monsters* mini-series for Marvel and *Joker's Asylum: Scarecrow* for DC. He is currently the artist for AMERICAN MONSTER with writer Brian Azzarello.

MARSHALL DILLON letterer
🐦 @MarshallDillon

A comic book industry veteran, Marshall got his start in 1994, in the midst of the indy comic boom. Over the years, he's been everything from an independent self-published writer to an associate publisher working on properties like *G.I.Joe, Voltron* and *Street Fighter.* He's done just about everything except draw a comic book, and worked for just about every publisher except the "big two." Primarily a father and letterer these days, he also dabbles in old-school paper & dice RPG game design. You can catch up with Marshall at firstdraftpress.net.